DATE DUE

DEC 1 3 '78			
JAN 2 7 '82			

A TIME TO SPEAK

A TIME TO SPEAK

By Charles Morgan, Jr.

HARPER & ROW, PUBLISHERS

NEW YORK,
EVANSTON,
AND LONDON

for my son, Charles

Contents

Preface

This book is about Americans, Southerners in a Southern city during a time of great social conflict. It tells the story of what happened—and what can happen—when the "decent" people of a community, Southern or Northern, remain silent too long while their nation's heritage of freedom is challenged.

The basis of twentieth-century totalitarianism wherever it flourishes is hatred and division among peoples, classes and races. The Nazis were a minority in Germany, just as the Communists are a minority in nations behind the Iron Curtain. But the totalitarians take power because the silent people of the middle, out of fear or indifference, do not stand up or speak up to block their way. In Germany, when it was all over, the "decent" burghers looked back at the bunkers and trench graves, ovens and lye, and the remains of millions of bodies and said: "We didn't know." What they meant was: "We didn't care enough to know."

A Time to Speak is a personal narrative. When a man travels a road that separates him from his community, the contributions of those who understand or who try to understand are doubly valued. To those friends who understood or, if they did not, at least tolerated; those who defended my right to dissent; those who stood by through the years—my thanks; to my parents, my brother and his family, who, whether agreeing or disagreeing with me, were my defenders, thanks. And most important of all, a special word of gratitude to my wife, Camille, who shared all of the experiences written of in this book and who helped me both live through them and set them to paper.

In relating the personal experiences in this book, I relied in large part on my recollection for bits of conversation and scraps of events. If any inaccuracies in recollection have occurred, I hope and trust they will be forgiven.

CHARLES MORGAN, JR.

Alexandria, Virginia
February, 1964

"A time to rend, and a time to sew; a time to
keep silence, and a time to speak."

ECCLESIASTES 3:7

A TIME TO SPEAK

The City of Churches

THE NOONTIME CARILLON played "Dixie." It was Monday, September 16, 1963. A warm Indian-summer smog hung heavy in the valley. And something else: an indefinable but thick human smog that seemed to slow the pace of the downtown lunch crowds, to muffle the usual clamor of the business district at peak of day.

This was to be the moment for silent prayer. "Birmingham," the *News* boasted, "has more than 700 churches and temples where weekly attendance is one of the highest in America." On Sunday one of those churches had been ripped open by dynamite. Four young girls, attending Sunday-school class, had died, and others had been maimed and mutilated. Jewish temples had twenty-four-hour armed guards protecting them now.

On Sunday night, as the shock wave of the day's atrocity

rolled through the valley and beyond, the mayor, the chief of police, the sheriff and a clergyman had appeared on television to call for civic calm and community prayer. "Wherever you may be at noon tomorrow," the clergyman said, "stop for a moment to bow your head in prayer during this hour of grief for our community and its people."

Mayor Boutwell asked for calm and restraint. The law-enforcement officers assured us that "the vile perpetrators of this dastardly deed" would be caught. We must pray and the guilty must be caught. Birmingham's "image" was in the balance.

Now it was noon Monday, and as I looked from my office window to the slow-moving city traffic below I remembered the clergyman's plea and thought to say a silent prayer. I recalled Chief Jamie Moore's stern pledge that "the guilty party or parties," whoever they might be, would be apprehended and brought before the bar of justice.

For more than eighteen years Birmingham had been my home. To others it was a problem, a recurrent blur of headlines, a flash of disaster. But to me it was home. That should have been enough. It wasn't.

How many hours had I spent working to build that medical center on the south side? That was the city's hope, an enterprise other than steel and coal and railroads. And it was expanding, bringing new people and research and the twentieth century to the city.

Here I was, thirty-three years old, in my ninth year of law practice. Those hours, days and months crisscrossing the state in one campaign or another; the late nights and long days on the phone or at meetings, hoping, working for change in the city and state; those long hours spent away from my son and my wife—where had they gone, what good had they done?

This was my home. There had been the presidency of the Junior Bar and the local Heart Association, the Advisory Committee on Schools, the State Mental Health Association's legislative chairmanship and that year when I was chairman of the Man of the Year Award. I had done those things a man should do at home. But what good had it done? All of the conflict and controversy of the city—I had been there but there was something strange about the place. It wouldn't change. Neither could I. And the burden of all those wasted years was with me now. I felt angry and very, very tired.

I watched the lunch crowds move and thought: the clergyman failed. It was noon in Birmingham, Alabama, and nobody stopped to pray. The noontime carillon played "Dixie," slowly. It was a dirge, not for the four who had died but for the city, and its sound rang through the valley and echoed back to the building top where the carillon played.

It was the Protective Life Building.

I left my office in the Bank for Savings Building. Just over a year ago I had watched the lighting ceremony that celebrated its completion. It was the first multi-story office building constructed in downtown Birmingham in three decades. At eight o'clock Labor Day evening the lights were to be turned on, ushering in a "new era" in city progress, according to the *News* and the Chamber of Commerce.

Automobiles had lined the streets for blocks and people stood on corners or craned their necks from car windows to watch. There were children and little old ladies, the "over-the-mountain" rich folks and the working folks from the steel mills, the rednecks from outlying rural areas and Negroes from Tuxedo Junction.

The lights went on. As each floor was lit in the beautiful new seventeen-story building, the crowd reacted with a murmur of awe. And it dawned on me that thousands of people had driven downtown on a muggy September night just to see a new building lit up. They were that hungry for a sign of progress. After thirty years they had their new building. The frustrations of decades were wrapped in the hope that those lights represented a "new era" for Birmingham.

With my wife, Camille, and our eight-year-old son, Charles, I had spent the day at an abandoned mining town on the Warrior River near Birmingham. Our host had spoken of the day, years ago, when the mine operators had stolen away, leaving behind them a community of unemployed mining families. And he had spoken at length of his dream of turning that now-deserted ghost town into a summer resort. We still had our dreamers in Birmingham. I suppose I was one of them. And so, after a hot and tiring day, we had hurried back to the city to the lighting of the building. I was to move my office to that building on the first night it opened for occupancy.

Now, a little more than a year later, I hurried away from the building, headed toward Twentieth Street and the retail shopping strip which, for some reason lost to the city's brief history, they called "The Racetrack." Little banners hung from lampposts proclaiming Birmingham's "Fall Fantasia." The merchants needed business. They had passed through a Negro boycott and later demonstrations when Negroes had charged into the streets, where they were met by police dogs and fire hoses. Now that they sold to Negroes they were beset by a white buyers' strike.

"Hard times come here first and leave here last," ran the often-heard local maxim. It wasn't an excuse, but a kind of civic boast. The Depression of the 1930's had hit Birmingham's single-industry steelmaking economy early and hung on late. In the thirties, Birmingham was brash and gaudy, but the Depression had left a deep psychic scar. Now there were few bright lights downtown at night, for the bright lights had grown dim years ago. And many of the bright minds had been driven away in those gray Depression years. It had been a brash city. Now it was simply sullen in its pride: "Hard times come here first and leave here last."

Nearby, on Morris Avenue, was the dental laboratory where my late father-in-law had worked for forty-two years. The building had been painted gray. There had been deaths there, but few other changes. Ed Porter, the Negro who had been my father-in-law's friend and employee for thirty years, still worked there. Ed did our yard work on weekends. Strange how his name wasn't Porter at all, but King. They started calling him Ed "Porter" to distinguish him from other Eds working there—the ones who weren't porters. The name stuck. That's the way it always was in Birmingham. Negroes are first-name people. Sometimes you know a wife's name or how many children they have. You know their last names if you pay them by check.

I walked past the giant First National Bank Building, a city landmark. It seemed to sit brooding at First Avenue and Twentieth Street, somehow disturbed that there were those who wanted their city to change. And past other buildings, structures that never changed, many of them owned by families that had long ago left Birmingham and Alabama; others owned by families whose absence might have given the

[5]

city a better opportunity to solve its problems. And past the ground-level parking lots. I remembered when a few years back a reporter for the *News* had written a lead to a downtown commercial development story: "Progress came once more to downtown Birmingham today with the opening of a gleaming new parking lot." In time the reporter, like anyone else who wrote or said things as he saw them, left the city. But his unpublished lead remained the truth about a community which, in an era of national and regional prosperity and expansion, had developed more ground-level parking lots than any like-size community in the country. While other cities grew tall, Birmingham tore down and leveled off.

The walk today, like all the other Monday walks to the Young Men's Business Club luncheon, was past the familiar faces of the news venders who, like the city itself, never seemed to change. Past the Twentieth Century Grill, where the young lawyers used to meet to talk of change and progress, and past Thompson's Restaurant, where you had the early-morning breakfasts after a football weekend party or an election night. Up Second Avenue, past Bromberg's and the Frank Nelson Building, past the Comer Building, where I had had my office for five years and John's Restaurant on Twenty-first Street, where the legal fraternity met to eat lunch and reargue the morning's court docket. John called me "Governor." He knew I liked the title.

And past the Presbyterian Church, and the Massey and Title buildings. This was the lawyers' street, Twenty-first, the road to the courthouse. It was the same drab street it had been eight years before, when I nervously walked the last mile to my first court case.

But it was at the corner of Fifth Avenue and Twenty-first Street that I saw the new force. Lining the street and around the corner were the parked blue-and-gray Fords of the Alabama State Highway Patrol.

After the settlement of the street demonstrations in May, bombs had exploded at the home of A. D. W. King and the Gaston Motel. Loss of life was only narrowly averted that wild Saturday night. The Negroes had rioted. They burned and ran amuck through the streets.

The State Patrol had come into Birmingham armed with carbines, tough, prepared for full-scale battle. From that night on they had become a new force. The Wallace administration had them equipped with steel helmets embossed with a small insignia: the Confederate battle flag. On the front bumper of each automobile there was, in metal, the same flag. Accompanied by a sheriff's posse from rural Dallas County and by employees of the State Conservation Department, they had made it known to the police of Birmingham and the local sheriff's office that they were taking charge. Their orders came from the governor. Even their organization's name had been changed. The words "State Troopers" were now emblazoned across the back of each automobile in yellow-and-black stick-on strips.

In the lobby of the Redmont Hotel there were twenty or thirty troopers laughing and talking. I walked through them and took an elevator to the second floor.

The city had been shocked by the Negro demonstrations in May. In a well-ordered and stratified community, disorder is the shock of shocks. Birmingham's citizens, baffled, annoyed, angered by the revelation that "our Southern Negroes" were in revolt, had reacted by defending everything, from the police dogs—"They were attacked by the demonstrators, you know"—to the high-powered fire hoses. But, no matter how often Birmingham blamed its problems on the "outside agitators," it somehow sensed that those who went to jail were local Negroes, their Negroes.

But the May violence had come and gone. To Birmingham, that tumultuous Saturday night four months past seemed eons ago.

Sluggings and beatings and bombing after bombing had inured Birmingham to violence and civic shock. There was to be no solution to the bombings. The residence of Arthur D. Shores, dean of Birmingham's Negro Bar, had twice been bombed. A fire bomb had struck the home of A. G. Gaston, the city's Negro millionaire. Only last week the Young Men's Business Club had pledged $250 to the city's reward fund. There had been such funds before, but they had led to the apprehension of no one. Yet the ritual of pledging had been a part of Birmingham's divestiture of guilt, a balm for the city's conscience.

Negro boycotts, repeated demands on the white community, successive waves of hope and disillusionment had molded a mass rationale for Greater Birmingham's 400,000 white citizens. Frustrated by past community failures, confounded by the accelerated pace of change and the violence it brought to the valley, Birmingham had learned to live with itself. It had learned to rationalize, to attack the accuser, to transfer guilt, to blame its troubles on "outside agitators" (the phrase was almost one word now), or the "niggers," or President Kennedy, or the Communists, or Martin Luther King, or the

Supreme Court. Afraid of violence but afraid to come to grips with its root causes, Birmingham went about its daily chores with the knowledge that, sooner or later, there would be another outbreak, another atrocity. "Things will get worse," people said, "before they get better."

And now the worst had happened. This Monday noon it was different. Everyone sensed it. They had come close before. They almost got those kids at the Bethel Baptist Church, the ones who were rehearsing for the Christmas pageant. But no one had been killed. Birmingham usually said that the "Negroes did it to themselves—after all, no one was killed." Today, the city did not say that—although one week later, after the first shock had passed, some would say it.

The members of the Young Men's Business Club were second-echelon executives, lawyers, newspapermen, engineers, architects, merchants, most of them in their late thirties. These were the future leaders of Birmingham, concerned about tomorrow. This was our home and we were trying to make it a better place to live for our children as well as ourselves. When action was needed to reapportion the rural-dominated state legislature, the YMBC's members filed the suit in federal court. YMBC members had been prime movers in the campaign to change the city's form of government, taking on Police Commissioner Eugene "Bull" Connor when older, wiser heads urged caution. And the club had made an effort to open community discussion of school desegregation, to face up to it as a community problem, not simply deal with it as a political issue. The fevered abuse of Birmingham's smear sheet artists was proof that the YMBC had been effective.

[9]

But, like the other good people of Birmingham, even the YMBC was a victim of the city's climate of fear. After all, there was just so much one group could do. Now the atrocity of atrocities had occurred in a community that prided itself on the number of its houses of worship and its high church attendance. In the City of Churches, four of God's children had been killed while attending Sunday school.

When the floor was opened for new business, a member stood up to introduce a resolution to condemn the bombings. And then someone else rose to speak of the damage inflicted on our community's "image." And so it was to be one more verbal condemnation of bombings, one more attempt to transfer guilt, one more chest-thumping resolution to hold together our city's image. Many times in recent years I had joined in such resolutions, helped draft them, argued for their adoption. But the time for whereases and wherefores, for the group therapy of resolution making—that time had run out. The time had come for someone to place the guilt where it had always belonged—not on the "outsiders" or the "hostile national press" or the Negro leaders or even the white supremacist extremists alone.

I had written the speech during the morning. It came from anger and despair, from frustration and empathy. And from years of hopes, hopes that were shattered and crumbled with the steps of that Negro Baptist Church.

"Four little girls were killed in Birmingham yesterday," it began. "A mad, remorseful, worried community asks, 'Who did it? Who threw that bomb? Was it a Negro or a white?' The answer should be 'We all did it.' Every last one of us is condemned for that crime and the bombing before it and the ones last month, last year, a decade ago. We all did it.

"A short time later, white policemen kill a Negro and wound another. A few hours later two young men on a motorbike shoot and kill a Negro child. Fires break out and, in Montgomery, white youths assault Negroes.

"And all across Alabama an angry, guilty people cry out their mocking shouts of indignity and say they wonder 'why?' 'who?' Everyone then 'deplores' the 'dastardly' act.

"But you know the 'who' of 'Who did it?' is really rather simple. The 'who' is every little individual who talks about the 'niggers' and spreads the seeds of his hate to his neighbor and his son. The jokester, the crude oaf whose racial jokes rock the party with laughter. The 'who' is every governor who ever shouted for lawlessness and became a law violator. It is every Senator and every Representative who in the halls of Congress stands and with mock humility tells the world that things back home aren't really like they are. It is courts that move ever so slowly and newspapers that timorously defend the law. It is all the Christians and all their ministers who spoke too late in anguished cries against violence. It is the coward in each of us who clucks admonitions. We are ten years of lawless preachments, ten years of criticism of law, of courts, of our fellow man; a decade of telling school children the opposite of what the civics books say. We are a mass of intolerance and bigotry and stand indicted before our young. We are cursed by the failure of each of us to accept responsibility, by our defense of an already dead institution.

"Yesterday while Birmingham, which prides itself on the number of its churches, was attending worship services, a bomb went off and an all-white police force moved into action, a police force which has been praised by city officials and others at least once a day for a month or so. A police force which has solved no bombings. A police force which many Negroes feel is perpetrating the very evils we decry. And why would Negroes think this?

"There are no Negro policemen: there are no Negro sheriff's deputies. Few Negroes have served on juries; few have been allowed to vote; few have been allowed to accept responsibility, or granted even a simple part to play in the administration of justice. Do not misunderstand me. It is not that I think that white policemen had anything whatsoever to do with the killing of these children or previous bombings. It's just that Negroes who see an all-white police force must think in terms of its failure to prevent or solve the bombings and think perhaps Negroes would have worked a little bit harder. They throw rocks and bottles and bullets. And we whites don't seem to know why the Negroes are lawless. So we lecture them.

"Birmingham is the only city in America where the police chief and the sheriff, in the school crisis, had to call our local ministers together to tell them to do their duty. The ministers of Birmingham who have done so little for Christianity call for prayer at high noon in a city of lawlessness and, in the same breath, speak of our city's 'image.' Did those ministers visit the families of the Negroes in their hour of travail? Did many of them go to the homes of their brothers and express their regrets in person or pray with the crying relatives? Do they admit Negroes into their ranks at the church?

"Who is guilty? A moderate mayor elected to change things

in Birmingham and who moves so slowly and looks elsewhere for leadership? A business community which shrugs its shoulders and looks to the police or perhaps somewhere else for leadership? A newspaper which has tried so hard of late, yet finds it necessary to lecture Negroes every time a Negro home is bombed? A governor who offers a reward but mentions not his own failure to preserve either segregation or law and order? And what of those lawyers and politicians who counsel people as to what the law is not, when they know full well what the law is?

"Those four little Negro girls were human beings. They had lived their fourteen years in a leaderless city; a city where no one accepts responsibility, where everyone wants to blame somebody else. A city with a reward fund which grew like Topsy as a sort of sacrificial offering, a balm for the consciences of the 'good people,' whose ready answer is for those 'right wing extremists' to shut up. People who absolve themselves of guilt. The liberal lawyer who told me this morning, 'Me? I'm not guilty,' he then proceeding to discuss the guilt of the other lawyers, the ones who told the people that the Supreme Court did not properly interpret the law. And that's the way it is with the Southern liberals. They condemn those with whom they disagree for speaking while they sit in fearful silence.

"Birmingham is a city in which the major industry, operated from Pittsburgh, never tried to solve the problem. It is a city where four little Negro girls can be born into a second-class school system, live a segregated life, ghettoed into their own little neighborhoods, restricted to Negro churches, destined to ride in Negro ambulances to Negro wards of hospitals or to a Negro cemetery. Local papers, on their front and editorial pages, call for order and then exclude their names from obituary columns.

"And who is really guilty? Each of us. Each citizen who has not consciously attempted to bring about peaceful compliance with the decisions of the Supreme Court of the United States, each citizen who has ever said 'they ought to kill that nigger,' every citizen who votes for the candidate with the bloody flag; every citizen and every school board member and school-teacher and principal and businessman and judge and lawyer who has corrupted the minds of our youth; every person in this community who has in any way contributed during the past several years to the popularity of hatred is at least as guilty, or more so, than the demented fool who threw that bomb.

"What's it like living in Birmingham? No one ever really has and no one will until this city becomes part of the United States.

"Birmingham is not a dying city. It is dead."

When I had finished, there was applause, and then one member rose. He suggested that we admit a Negro into the club. There was silence. The motion died. Soon the Young Men's Business Club of Birmingham, Alabama, adjourned its meeting of September 16, 1963.

It was one o'clock. Downstairs the troopers still laughed and talked, and blocks away the carillon again played "Dixie."

CHAPTER

II

Peace in the Valley

The sign in front of the Terminal Station proclaimed "The Magic City." It was 1945. We had come to make our home in Birmingham, Alabama.

The "magic" lay in the city's quick growth, from a quiet village to a major Southern metropolis in one industrial leap. Sheltered by Red Mountain, which separated its soot and its society, Birmingham was at night afire with the workings of steel. It was big. It was young. There was no antebellum Birmingham, no memory of Appomattox.

For our family Birmingham represented opportunity for my father, the greener pasture of the transferred American businessman, the breed who had grown with the automobile and radio and selling and two world wars, during which men saw new places, new land and new opportunity.

We had come from Fort Thomas, Kentucky, a peaceful

little residential community far from picket lines and soup kitchens. During the 1930's and the early war years the last house on East Southgate Avenue was home to me. Seven acres of woods overlooking the Ohio River valley. A place where a boy could stand and see an airport, in the days when men still traveled by railroad and marveled over aircraft; a flood, like the one in 1937; or a river upon which barges moved and which, when winter came, might be a mass of ice. This was my little part of Kentucky, and Kentucky was the whole world to me.

My father grew up in the mountain country up around Prestonburg, Kentucky. Born near Lackey "up on Beaver Creek," he had worked for every penny he spent and every lesson he learned. By the time I was born he had come a long way from the ten cents a day he made as a youth pushing fallen timber away from creek banks and back into the main stream. He fought his way out of those mountains in the early 1900's, traveling a road that led through work on the farm, in tobacco fields, then to teaching and selling.

Then, just before the outbreak of World War I, he went to work for the insurance company that he would stay with the remainder of his business life, more than forty years. He met my mother in Paducah, Kentucky, where she had been born. They were married in 1924 in Gulfport, Mississippi. I was born on March 11, 1930.

My mother's grandmother had remembered and recounted to her as a child the legendary Southern family stories of "burying the silver when the Yankees came." The folk heritage of the Civil War grew to be a part of my mother's life and mine. With these memories we became Confederates in the same strange way known to all the descendants of a vanquished generation.

Mother had grown up in the world of colored help. Her nursemaid had been her mother's nursemaid, Aunt Edie. She was an old woman when Mother was a child, and about all she did was look after Mother and the other children and tell them her own animal stories. After Aunt Edie had become terribly involved in her lore, when there was no possible ending or out for all of the characters she had created, when the children were all asking, "What happened then, Aunt Edie, what happened then?" the old woman would end by saying, "Oh, oh, 'bout dat time de bell rung and I lef'!" Everyone loved Aunt Edie and, as Mother told me, she was taken care of until she died.

And, in Mother's life, there was Ella, the cook and maid, who bossed everyone. There was Uncle Alvin, the yardman, houseman, handyman. There was Annie, who came in to help clean and help with the laundry. Annie brought her three smallest children with her—triplets named Tee, Mike and Soda. And Mother and the other children played with them. That was the way it was in Paducah while Mother was growing up.

In Fort Thomas during the Depression years there was relative prosperity. And, for me and my brother, John, there was the uncomplicated world of baseball, football and basketball; of the collections of cards that came with chewing gum, of garages or, in the country, barns sporting a rim and net, or perhaps a bushel basket or a barrel hoop and a small boy shooting with a ball or a bundle of rags.

Kentucky was the state where Lincoln and Jefferson

Davis were born. It was a place of politics and battle and a heritage of divided homes and families during the Civil War. Where my mother lived it had been Confederate territory. Where my father lived it was split. In the mountains where my father lived there were few Negro families. Where Mother lived there were many.

Through the early years there were the South and Southern folklore in our home and in our school. Mother liked the third-grade teacher, but she could never quite forgive her for trying to take away my Southern accent.

There was Irene Logan—maid, confidante, cook, washer and ironer. She worked for us for all those childhood years. And perhaps in knowing her there were the seeds of the dissent of another time and place. Irene looked out for us. She was a "member of the family," as Mother used to say. Irene made us mind, she fed us and she laughed.

There were some things about which a small boy wondered. Why did Irene have her own bathroom? Why did she have her own glass and plate?

There were stories Irene told about how the Negroes in Covington and Newport tore parts of their new housing projects away and used them as kindling for fires. And I remembered talk about the days when Negroes in Cincinnati went to town to bump white people off the street. But the important stories were those of how my father would fire insurance men who were rude to Negroes. And how he shook hands with Negroes.

Mother, with her Southern accent, always played the part of the Negro Mammy in the local little-theater group. Her reminiscences carried with them the Southern dreams of honor. As Mother said, no "true Southerner" ever mistreated a slave and no true Southerner would ever mistreat a Negro. She would say of some of her friends, "They just don't know how to handle their colored help." Mother and Daddy always called them "colored" but never "nigger." The word "nigger" was the language of poor white trash, a language we never heard in our home. If Mother's loyalty to a "Southern way of life" was loyalty to a myth, she never was to know it. Father had a sense of loyalty, too. Loyalty to Mother, to his sons, to his company, to his men and to his country.

Daddy loved this country. He had done well in it. His father had died when he was very young. As a small boy he was reared with brothers and sisters and half brothers and sisters and stepbrothers and sisters in a mountain home. He told of making soap and going to town in the fall to buy his annual pair of shoes. He told of walking all those miles through snow and rain to learn to read and write. The country had been good to Daddy.

He was a sensitive man. How I remember Sunday dinner, December 7, 1941. Father was never profane in front of my brother, John, and me. But that Sunday, when he heard the news, he was profane and he meant it. He got sick and couldn't eat.

My father never worried about a man's religion. He didn't seem to have a prejudice. When I was young he told me about how he, a Baptist, voted for Al Smith. He left the Democrats to join the Willkie movement, but never was I to hear him speak ill of a man's race or religion. There was never an eyebrow raised or a word uttered about a child's

name. It didn't matter whether it was Mansberg or Mc-
Farland or Sarakasanis. No Negroes lived in Fort Thomas.

There were trips to the Zoo and Coney Island and to the
swimming pools and Cincinnati. There was supper at Mills
Cafeteria (I preferred the Dixie Chili Parlor) and there were
the Art Museum, the symphony and the occasional road show
that came to the city, across the river.

There in the quiet of a small town my brother and I grew
up in the world of the secure.

But I was fifteen years old now and we were moving to
Birmingham, The Magic City.

Within the lifetime of men then living, seventy-five years,
an engineer named Milner had made a deal with a promoter
from Boston named Stanton. Out of this deal and the promoter's double-cross grew Birmingham.

Milner was promoting interest in a railroad that the Confederates had planned but failed to complete. Stanton was
building another railroad across Alabama to Chattanooga.
The roads were to join in a mineral-rich Alabama valley. It
was there that Milner and Stanton planned their town site.
Not far away was the village of Elyton. Stanton deceitfully
changed his right-of-way so that his railroad would pass closer
to Elyton. He then proceeded to take options on nearby land.
Milner, undaunted by this perfidy, simply slowed construction until Stanton's land options expired and then picked
up the options. Thus the birth, on January 26, 1871, of
the Elyton Land Company (its direct descendant is today's
Birmingham Realty Company). They named their gamble
Birmingham.

They had it made the seat of Jefferson County, and the outsiders began to arrive. There were minerals here, everyone soon knew that, and with these minerals there was a fortune to be made.

The railroad, having no northern connection, foundered, but was saved by the Louisville and Nashville line.

Across the land fortunes were being made, industrial empires created. From its iron and steel Birmingham was to be built on the ruins of a state ravaged by war, impoverished and largely populated by illiterate and poor Negroes and whites.

Then came the panic of 1873, and for the first of many times in its history Birmingham was hit early and hurt long. As the nation revived, so did Birmingham. Its promoters bought and sold, opened mines, developed communities, and the area grew in the form of a wheel of fortune. The hub was Birmingham, the home office for the promoters who then lived on the side of Red Mountain. Around the city grew its plants, and beyond them, burrowing into the earth's innards, were the mines.

This was the time for creation of Birmingham's old family dynasties. It was a Henry DeBardeleben who organized iron and coal and land and established towns and villages. It was an Enoch Ensley who named his settlement and the Bank of Ensley, and when his bubble burst sold out for $16,000.

In 1886 there came the Tennessee Coal, Iron and Railroad Company. Even then, T.C.I. was New York controlled; the DeBardelebens and the Ensleys owned a piece of it. And now Birmingham was on its way to the future, plunging hellbent toward a tomorrow which would include forty-eight Alabama lynchings in the two-year period 1891-1892.

The city's founding fathers adopted the strident political

intonations of the day. White supremacy became a rallying cry, and Joseph F. Johnston, former president of Sloss Iron and Steel Company, was elected governor of Alabama. In 1901, the Constitution of Alabama was written. Its authors' eyes were on the complete elimination of the Negro from the voter rolls. The new Constitution provided for an apportionment of the state legislature that was to place Alabama permanently in the hands of rural "Black Belt" interests who, for the next sixty years, were to control the lives and fortunes of the state and its people.

In 1907 the United States Steel Corporation acquired T.C.I. Control of the city's economy was now locked in the hands of Northerners. The Louisville and Nashville and the Southern railroads had both looked North for investors and the newly formed Alabama Power Company was soon to become a subsidiary of the Commonwealth and Southern Corporation. Freight rate differentials were locked in place and Birmingham became a Southern industrial stepchild to Northern financial interests.

Soon came the city's first wave of labor violence. In 1908, meeting in woods, taking obligations in gullies by candlelight, the United Mine Workers organized. Twenty thousand whites and Negroes went out on strike. The Tennessee Company moved quickly to smash the movement. The strikers were dispossessed and shabby tent villages sprang up throughout the valley. Then came lynchings, strike breakers and convict labor. The use of the convict labor system with its filthy work camps, disease and death was not to be abolished until mid-1928. And again the cry of "nigger, nigger." Governor Comer, the cotton mill man whose name was to adorn the city's tallest building, sent in the National Guard. The Mine Workers' national vice-president ended the strike.

The city evolved into a repository for the tough and ignorant, for men who worked with their backs and hands and muscle. Little thought was given to their education or their children's or to the sewer system in the mining towns or to the mortality rate of miners.

Birmingham was a crucible of all the forces that breed violence: poor and impoverished whites and Negroes; an economy controlled in the North; a political and economic system based on the blood and sweat of workers whose lives were made up of fists and knives, guns and dynamite, Saturday-night whiskey, and chits at the company store.

But to others Birmingham was a city to be saved, a call to bravery for the few like Julia Strudwick Tutwiler and Samuel Ullman, or for a Christian like Brother Bryan. Birmingham was and always had been a calendar of conflict, a place of promise, of romance and writing, of complacency and of fear.

Now, in 1945, Birmingham was no longer a city of promoters and speculators. The control of minerals had long since gone to others. Upon a pioneer foundation of bigotry and hatred there had been built a community led by corporate executives and salesmen of goods and services. Birmingham was to sell life and burial insurance and automobiles, steel and pipe. And, from a bitter past, it looked ahead to the achievement of community promise that forever seemed within reach, but was never quite fulfilled.

How was Birmingham to know that steel and railroads

were not to be the romance industries of another day?

Birmingham in 1945 was a city the gamblers had left. And while other cities borrowed and built and gambled on their future, Birmingham settled down, prosperous and happy.

And to teen-agers in fashionable suburban Mountain Brook, where I was now to live, Birmingham meant Florida in the summertime and football in the fall. It meant the Pickwick Club, where the young ladies from the fine families were ending their childhood, dancing the hours away. And while they danced the "Birmingham Hop" time slipped by.

Who could see fifteen years ahead? Who could sense the problems of a later day? The war was over and there was peace in the valley.

CHAPTER

III

From Campus to Campaign

THE UNIVERSITY OF ALABAMA at Tuscaloosa is the cap-
stone of state politics as well as education. Over the years a
political tradition has grown up about the campus and at
one point in recent years more Alabama alumni held seats
in the U.S. Senate than could be claimed by the university of
any other state. Their philosophies ranged from that of East-
land of Mississippi to that of Pepper of Florida. Native sons
Lister Hill and John J. Sparkman cut their political teeth
on Alabama student government politics, and—although
the state no longer claims it—Mr. Justice Hugo La Fayette
Black came out of the red clay hills of East Alabama to work
his way through the university.

I had grown up amidst talk of politics as had, perhaps,
everyone whose early years were spent in Kentucky. My interest may have started with marking my father's paper ballot
when he took me to the polls or the fervor in the chant, "We

want Willkie!" when I was ten. I suppose an interest in politics is caught, not learned. At any rate, I had two primary interests: law and politics.

My parents wanted me to go to college in the East, but with an eye to a future career in Alabama I held out for the state university. There friendships and allegiances were to be formed, and, in the years ahead, these would be the good old days to remember and relive with classmates and contemporaries. These are the school ties that bind in the politics of Alabama, and somehow I sensed this even then.

The Alabama campus encapsulates the dominant power structure of the state at large. In 1947, though a large number of students were from out of state, the school remained a Deep Southern institution with a Deep Southern outlook. Alabama's race problem was still a matter for theoretical discussion at late-night bull sessions, and the only racial controversy I recall during my first years on campus concerned whether Satchmo Armstrong's band could make a personal appearance at a student dance. The student body voted yes, but the school administration at the time ruled it out.

There was, however, one heated controversy that led to a week of night-time demonstrations on campus. These occurred when Alabama's winning Crimson Tide of 1950 was spurned by the Orange Bowl in Miami. I served as a one-man telephone committee to bring out the crowds in protest. I was so successful, having a popular cause, that finally the Dean of Men braced me on campus one afternoon with a pointed question. "Tell me, *Mister* Morgan," he asked. "What time is the *spontaneous* demonstration scheduled to begin tonight?"

Five years later student demonstrations of a far different

nature were to rock the campus, protesting the admission of Autherine Lucy to the university.

In the one-party Deep South, where personality rather than organization is the determining factor in politics, state political leaders keep a close, often wary, eye on student government comers at the state university. My first exposure to the real world of Alabama politics came during the Democratic primary for governor in spring, 1950. I had visited the summer home of Gordon Persons, then an Alabama Public Service Commissioner, in Florida. I knew his son, and for those on the periphery of political life the chance meeting or the speaking acquaintanceship draws like a magnet. I was asked to help and I did. The experience confirmed my judgment that an Eastern college was no place for a young man with his mind set on entering Alabama politics. I learned a great deal in a brief two months of stump speaking for my gubernatorial candidate around Tuscaloosa County, the chief lesson being that the practice of politics in Alabama sometimes has as much to do with show business as with public affairs.

There were fifteen candidates for governor in the primary and most of them visited the campus during the course of the campaign. One North Alabama candidate blew onto University Avenue one bright morning, driving a railroad locomotive on rubber wheels. Another addressed the student body from a flat truck specially designed, at high cost, to simulate the state capitol in Montgomery.

But little that occurred in the 1950 gubernatorial campaign was to prepare a young university student for the

storm that lay ahead. Segregation as an issue played no part
in the final results, in which the helicopter candidate, Gordon
Persons, was elected. Birmingham Police Commissioner Eugene Connor, who tried to make it an issue, ran far down the
list of fifteen candidates.

To a political-minded undergraduate, certain flesh-and-
blood public figures emerge as models to emulate, heroes of
a kind. Three men were to have an important influence on
my attitude toward politics and the issues of the times, one
a national figure and two state leaders.

The national figure was Adlai Stevenson. As national com-
mitteeman for the Alabama League for Young Democrats, I
once again took to the stump in Tuscaloosa and surrounding
counties to speak for the Stevenson-Sparkman ticket in 1952.
It was during this campaign that I first came up against the
barbs of the race issue. In 1948, Alabama had left the national
Democratic party to support the Thurmond-Wright ticket.
Although by 1952 the state faction loyal to the national party
had regained control of party machinery, resentment against
the Truman civil rights program still had Alabama Democrats on the defensive. The Alabama Republican party
adroitly attacked the national Democratic party as being anti-
Southern, and although Stevenson carried the state the campaign was a portent of future trouble. Most of my friends
in Birmingham's over-the-mountain suburbs supported General Eisenhower, whose chief political attraction for the area
—or so it seemed to me—was that he had no debatable record
on the race issue.

The two state leaders whom I came to admire were totally
different in style, one being the greatest mass appeal politi-

cian in Alabama history, the other being a man who applied his political energies behind the scenes. But both had one thing in common: regard for the Negro as a human being.

When James E. Folsom was rounding out his first term as governor, he devoted part of his 1949 official Christmas message to the race issue—but in a way few Alabama officials, before or since, have had the courage to do. It was a simple statement, hardly courageous had it been spoken by the governor of a Northern or Eastern state; but considering Alabama's political atmosphere, it was a bombshell.

"As long as the Negroes are held down by deprivation and lack of opportunity," Governor Folsom said, "the other poor people will be held down alongside them. Let's start talking fellowship and brotherly love, and do unto others. Let's do more than talk about it. Let's start living it."

"Big Jim" (he was six feet eight inches tall) had attended the University but never graduated. Born and reared in the wire-grass section of Southeast Alabama, he had twice run for Congress and twice been defeated. He packed his bags and moved to North Alabama, his political instincts sharpened by the influence of WPA and a Depression-racked farm country. He first ran for governor in 1942 and lost.

In 1946 he was not considered a major contender by state political leaders. They, the daily newspapers and industrial spokesmen, who habitually selected the governor, had chosen sides and were looking to others for the contest. Big Jim was written off as an outsized freak with radical ideas and a roughneck rural following. But Folsom didn't seem to care about the political leaders, and he made no overtures to industry. He had built the semblance of an organization during his 1942 campaign. It was the people of the branch heads and their relatives working in the mills and mines he depended on for victory.

Like no Alabama politician before him, Folsom could draw a crowd. As if his height weren't enough, he hired a string band, named it the "Strawberry Pickers," and with a mop and "suds bucket" in tow he hied off across the state, making six, eight or ten stops a day, speaking at every country crossroads. He was going to "mop up that mess down there in Montgomery."

White-suited, thirty-seven years old, Folsom indeed looked like an undignified buffoon to the nice people, and they laughed at him. But, out in the country, away from telephones and electricity and paved roads, the farmers were listening to Jim. They came to town to hear him. Star-route box holders got announcements of his speaking engagements and they came. They shuffled their feet in time to the country music and laughed some, not much. There was little applause. They listened.

He told them how their state government was run by the industrial interests of Birmingham and the North and East. He called those interests the "Big Mules" and the "Gotrocks," and in the classic Populist tradition of the South he waged political war against the rich city folk. He told the farmers that dirt roads would disappear if he got elected and that they would travel to market on paved highways. He talked of how the Black Belt plantation owners and the Big Mules were running the state. Folsom spoke of the dreams of the little man, of the worker and the farmer, and they listened. He spoke of pensions for the aged. He told them he remembered as a small boy lying in bed in the morning at sun-up and breathing that "clean, fresh, green breeze that comes across the fields." He told them that was what he was going to take to Montgomery with him, that "clean, fresh, green breeze."

He told them his campaign needed money and passed them the "suds bucket," and they gave.

He told the ladies he wanted to kiss them and they let him.

He attacked the big daily newspapers ("them lyin' dailies") and they photographed him. And when he gained strength and they stopped printing his remarks and pictures, he lay down on courthouse steps and they photographed him.

They said he was a puppet of Sidney Hillman and the C.I.O. Political Action Committee. He asked for the votes of the working man.

And he never profaned the Negroes. He shook their hands and asked for votes.

The people listened and they voted. They came from the little towns and villages, from off creek banks and out of the fields, and they voted. They voted for a hope and a promise, the dream of a better life. "Old Jim tells 'em, don't he?" "Ain't he somethin'?" He told us to come to the inauguration and I'm a-goin'." "He ain't got no campaign manager here so I'm just goin' to ask him for that road he promised me."

To a college student who was interested in politics, Folsom was troubling. He continued to talk of his dreams of reapportionment. He attacked the poll tax and restrictions on voting.

Folsom changed the state's politics much as did television. He took talk directly to the people. Never again were the daily newspapers, the Big Mules, and the Black Belt to rest easy.

My mother shook her head, my father grumbled to himself about the worth of sending a boy off to college for a higher education—but I went out and worked for Folsom.

The other state political personality who made a deep impression on my evolving political attitudes was a heavy-set, quiet-spoken Tuscaloosa attorney they called "Foots." From the time I first contemplated going to law school and entering political life I had heard of Marc Ray Clement as a man to meet. Finally I did meet him when, as the university's homecoming chairman in 1950, I went to his office in downtown Tuscaloosa to ask him to judge the contest for homecoming queen.

"I'd like to help you out," he said, smiling wryly, "but I know too many of the fathers involved. No matter whose daughter I helped select, ten others would be mad at me for life."

I told him that my trip downtown wasn't a complete loss, since he was a man I had wanted to know. He laughed, put his large-size shoes on his desk top, and started talking, slowly, measuring out every word and thought. He talked of politics with the affectionate pride of a man who enjoyed his participation in the democratic process. He told me of his days at the university, of the Congressmen who were his classmates, and of Alabama's two Senators. And he spoke, with anything but the cool detachment I might have expected from a professional politician, of his belief in the Tennesse Valley Authority, the Hill-Burton hospital act, Franklin D. Roosevelt and the New Deal.

Foots was a loyal Democrat and he minced no words when discussing the Dixiecrat movement in the South.

"Loyalty is the most important thing you'll learn in life

and in politics," he told me. "Loyalty to principles and loyalty to friends. If you want to be successful in politics, tie yourself to your principles and your friends, and if you're for the right things, you and the principles you believe in will scale the mountain." He leaned forward and tapped his desk with a finger, emphasizing each word. "Let me tell you something, Chuck," he said. "When you stick by what you believe and don't change, that rope gets tough as a chain and it can't be broken."

As I got up to leave, he rose and we shook hands. "And one more thing," he said. "Don't ever agree to be a judge in a college beauty contest."

In the years ahead Foots Clement was to advise and counsel me about my future and to bring me into campaign and Democratic party circles. For he was the man in Alabama who kept political details straight, advised and listened to politicians, searched for young men for their organizations, and tried to apply his influence to keep the state on a moderate and progressive course.

Foots wasn't a Folsom supporter, but he differed from Big Jim more in method than in political philosophy. Both were devoted to the people they served and to the Democratic party. Foots died in 1961. He had won his fight against the Dixiecrats, but he left the scene at a time when the Democrats of Alabama were taking an even more dangerous direction, away from the party loyalty he believed was best for the state and the country.

In September of 1953 Camille and I were married in Tuscaloosa in Canterbury chapel. We had dated for several years. George M. Murray, the Episcopal chaplain who had become our close friend during those college years, officiated. Nine years later he was to be Bishop Co-adjutor of the Diocese of Alabama and we were to speak, in a crowded Chamber of Commerce auditorium, of the certain-to-come integration of Birmingham schools. But now he was performing our marriage in a chapel we had grown to love and it was an end to my salad days of Orange Bowl demonstrations.

We lived in a small converted barracks-type university apartment. You could see the ground through the floor and it was too hot in the summer, too cold in winter. But it was inexpensive and our first home. Camille worked as a secretary for the university and I got a job teaching American Economic History. In this way we met most of the family bills.

In 1953, State Senator Albert Boutwell of Birmingham was named chairman of the legislative committee to study methods of keeping Alabama's schools segregated. The issue which Southern historian Ulrich B. Phillips called the "central theme of Southern history" was not yet dominant in the state's politics, but it was slowly rising to the surface, in anticipation of Supreme Court decisions to come. I felt the gathering momentum of the segregation issue as a member of the Alabama delegation to the Young Democrats national convention at St. Paul, Minnesota, that same year. Though I didn't know it at the time, I was to come face to face with it in the person of the leader of our state delegation, a young, hard-driving Folsom lieutenant named George Corley Wallace who had just recently been elected circuit judge of his home county in South Alabama.

The overwhelming majority of Alabama delegates to the

1953 St. Paul Young Democrats convention were opposed to the Adlai Stevenson faction of the party. A Stevenson vs. anti-Stevenson issue was to take form in the election of a national president for the Young Democrats.

The Stevenson candidate was Neal Smith of Iowa, now a Congressman. Members of our delegation threw their support behind Smith's opponent from Indiana. The convention began with its traditional row over which delegation from Texas was to be seated. As a member of the credentials committee, I voted for the faction that was pro-Stevenson, to the chagrin of my fellow Alabamians.

Alabama was to yield to Indiana to allow the nomination of the anti-Stevenson man. But Wallace determined to find out how the Indiana candidate stood on civil rights. Following a caucus the Indianian failed to support a strong civil rights resolution, although his delegation favored it. I went to Wallace and asked him directly how he could back a man for the national Presidency who allowed his entire delegation to vote one way while he voted another. Shortly after that, "The Little Judge," as Wallace liked to be called, concluded he couldn't vote for either Smith or the Indianian. The Alabama delegation nominated and voted for a favorite son from Slocomb, Alabama. George Wallace got to make a speech; Stevenson's man was elected. Everybody returned home satisfied, little realizing that we had taken part, on a minor league scale, in a deadly political game that would soon involve every politician in Alabama and would be played in the major league of national senior party conventions. The segregation trap—or "Seg," as it came to be called—had warped and inhibited our delegation's every action at St. Paul. And

George Wallace, a young politician whose record in the legislature had earned him a reputation as a liberal, was among its first victims.

The following spring of 1954 I was to watch Wallace in action as South Alabama campaign manager for Big Jim Folsom's second gubernatorial campaign. On the Saturday night before the primary I traveled to Birmingham with Camille to see Folsom climax his stump speaking tour with a rally in front of the Jefferson County courthouse. The candidate was preceded by three of his prophets of the Grange, each raising a crowd of several thousand to a new plateau of excitement. It was marvelous show business and, as the election results of the following Tuesday were to prove, the best politics.

First came George Hawkins, the North Alabama campaign manager from Gadsden, rousing the crowd of upstate farmers from underrepresented counties with a call for legislative reapportionment. Then came The Little Judge, berating the "Gotrock" interests who fought Big Jim's progressive program for the people of Alabama. And then came Rankin Fite, legislator from Northwest Alabama, who brought the audience to frenzied, foot-stomping indignation at the vile tactics of the "big city newspapers" who were against Big Jim. Finally Folsom came on, while his "Corn Grinders" band played a medley of backwoods campaign tunes. He damned the "divisive forces" in the state, called for everyone to come together in an era of good feeling and progress for Alabama.

Folsom was to win in a landslide. Three weeks later, the Supreme Court ruled in the case of *Brown, et al. vs. Board of Education of Topeka, et al.,* and with that decision the era

Big Jim promised would be stillborn. The temper of the state's campaigns, the very political personalities of its participants would be altered by the impact of the dominant and foreboding political issue of a new era. Wallace would come to power eight years later on the issue that his mentor spurned. Fite would become House floor leader for the Wallace administration. Hawkins would become president pro tem of the State Senate.

I was graduating. Seven years of campus life had brought me the two degrees, the ODK key, the law school honors, the campus leadership and the contacts I had set out to get when I first entered the university. And more, much more, as the passage of time would prove.

There was the lasting influence of the professors. Not all the professors, of course, but the special few who have the gift of making yesterday, today and even tomorrow come alive to the young but directionless mind: the professor of Latin American history who regularly mounted his podium and strode across the Andes—Bolívar, San Martín, José Marte came alive in a mid-twentieth-century classroom in Tuscaloosa, Alabama; the political science teacher who gave form and meaning to the concept of democratic government; and the law professors who worked to infuse in students not simply the categories and rules of our legal system, but the significance of the struggle for the rights of man. These were the men who taught me to regard people as people rather than contacts—and that perhaps was the biggest lesson I learned during those seven years.

But there was also a lesson in tragedy to be learned at the university. Autherine Lucy, Negro, had applied for admission. The seeds of disaster for the South and nation were being sown.

The lesson: in their failure to speak and act at every stage of crisis, the moderates—the nice, good, safe, respectable people—bear the major share of responsibility for the acts of violent men in the street.

Louisiana State University and the University of North Carolina had desegregated without violence and disorder. Convinced that the Lucy admission could be equally uneventful I went to Dr. Oliver Cromwell Carmichael, one of the country's leading educators, and told him of my interest in working for campus acceptance of the Lucy admission. Dr. Carmichael was courteous and thanked me for my interest. I was not to hear from him again.

Despite ingrained Alabama attitudes toward segregation, the Lucy riots of 1956 were not inevitable. As a matter of fact, only an incredible series of oversights, miscalculations and blunders in Washington, Montgomery and Tuscaloosa made it possible for a small minority of university students—joined by a ragtail group of off-campus toughs—to successfully thwart orders of a federal court.

The Lucy case had been pending in the courts for years. But, when the time for her entry to the school eventually came, the university was woefully unprepared. I had graduated and was to read in the *News* of the wild crowds which rocked the automobiles of Negroes driving down University Avenue and ran in the streets. But in far-off Washington no action was taken to enforce the orders of the United States court. In Montgomery no plans had been made nor had effective action been taken to maintain order on the state university campus.

The Autherine Lucy demonstrations were to open a long night of violence not only for Alabama but for the South. In Little Rock a year from then, at Oxford and later at Tuscaloosa, the course of the Lucy appeasement was to be seen. Had the state's nice people sought to prepare the way for desegregation and had state and federal authority been brought to bear in Tuscaloosa immediately, the destructive forces rampant in school desegregation cases might have been nipped in the bud.

In the end whatever niceties of administrative policy led to Autherine Lucy's dismissal, the rioters appeared to have won the battle of the streets. The lesson seemed clear enough and its message flashed across the South: Violence works.

The "moderates" who remained silent and did nothing to assure a place for moderation in the state had lost a key battle to the militant extreme. Now, for the first time in Alabama, White Citizens Council groups began to spring up everywhere. And, as they would so many times in future years, the decent, law-abiding people of the state settled upon a comfortable explanation of how the Lucy riots had come about: everything would have been all right, they told each other, if the NAACP hadn't driven her down to Tuscaloosa dressed fit to kill—and in a big black Cadillac.

When she finally left Alabama, Autherine Lucy told the press that her one moment of hope had come some time before her violent entry on campus, while her case was still pending. A student leader had called and told her he would try his best to help prepare her way onto campus. I read her farewell comment with interest and a degree of regret for a battle lost. I had been the caller.

CHAPTER

IV

Law and the Order

For a brief while I thought of staying to teach at the university, but the combat of the courtroom and the stump awaited. I was offered a chance to go to work as a lawyer for the state, but knew that my course was set for returning to Birmingham to take up law—and politics.

We moved from Tuscaloosa to Birmingham under our own power. With the help of our families and Ed Porter, we managed to transfer our earthly possessions in confusion—and a rented truck.

My starting salary with the law firm wasn't much, $250 per month, but the apartment rent was geared to the young. And our new neighbors were in many instances old friends from college beginning their business and professional careers. No one seemed to care about outdoing the neighbors; at least we didn't.

On Saturday nights we cooked out back and had our

parties. The women talked of babies (someone's new one was always on the way or had just arrived), maids, clothes and the latest minor scandal. And the men spoke of politics—they were all Republicans—of their work and of football. On football we could agree.

But slowly we all became a part of the suburban life. With each raise in salary there grew an interest in real-estate advertisements in the Sunday *News,* and the young women began to drive in search of homes in Mountain Brook with just enough grass to create a problem for their husbands. And the men searched for more time for golf and more money from work.

One by one we were all to move from the apartments into our own homes and the communications between us would fade into memories; but for now we were happy and young and searching for success.

The firm I had gone to work for lived in the antiseptic legal world of administrative proceedings, municipal bonds, proxy contests and corporate problems.

Many lawyers never enter a criminal courtroom. They stitch and mend and patch the fabric of society but they avoid the arena where death waits in the wings. They have read of Darrow and the great trials of the past but for top graduates of law school the jump to the security of a corporate firm and a specialty is both easy and comfortable.

In Birmingham hundreds of men went to jail each year without even conversing with an attorney. The Supreme Court of the United States had not yet ruled that all men charged with a felony were entitled to counsel. And in Alabama the state law merely required that lawyers be appointed to defend those whose cases might result in the imposition of the death penalty. In order to be appointed to defend an accused pauper the lawyer must attend court on arraignment day and wait his turn.

I supposed that a lawyer who had never handled a criminal case had never really done his job, and for better or for worse I wanted to experience a criminal trial. Most of the lawyers who were appointed to defend indigents were young and in-experienced and, if the client suffered, the lawyer learned and earned. But he didn't earn much considering that a life was in the balance. Under Alabama law, the fee for a young lawyer defending an indigent client accused of an offense punishable by death was $100—"Win, lose or draw," as an older attorney had explained.

I asked the senior partners of our firm for permission to defend a pauper. Permission was granted.

Before the bench of Circuit Judge Robert Wheeler came the dregs of Birmingham. On capital arraignment day the defendants were seated, racially segregated and handcuffed, to the right of the bench. On the judge's left, in the jury box, sat the lawyers. In front, at counsels' table, was the deputy circuit solicitor. And beyond the rail, to the rear of the room, were the families and friends of the accused, segregated by a center aisle.

Judge Wheeler was a stern man who went straight to the day's docket with little wasted motion.

"Do you have a lawyer, Henry?" he asked a tall, gasping Negro whose indictment for first degree murder had just been read to the court.

"Nawsah," Henry replied. I looked closely at the man as he stood before the bench. He sucked in his breath and seemed to choke with each word. My immediate impression was that he was destined to be found guilty, and worse yet I couldn't contain the thought that he indeed looked guilty of something.

"Do you have any money?"

The question was purely pro forma. It was clear that Henry had nothing—not even a relative or a friend in the courtroom.

"Mr. Morgan will be your lawyer, Henry," said the judge, and my first client sat down stiffly as the next defendant's name was called and the wheels of justice ground ahead.

Before my first interview with Henry I went by the coroner's office on the sixth floor of the courthouse.

"That's one nigger they ought to *throw* in the electric chair," the coroner told me. "Understand, he didn't just *kill* that woman, he hit her so hard with a shotgun barrel it knocked her *eyeballs* out."

My informant shook his head dolefully. "That wouldn't have been so bad," he continued, " 'cept he *stabbed* her three hours before that with a butcher knife just 'cause she wouldn't cook him breakfast."

He paused as I took notes. "This your first capital case?" he asked. I nodded. He shook his head again. "I guess you know," he said, "she was a widow woman with four kids on welfare." I kept writing. "Paralyzed at that," he went on remorselessly, "paralyzed from head to foot on her right side."

"Where, and when," I finally summoned up courage to ask, "did it happen?"

It had happened at high noon in full view of twelve eye witnesses.

I had been right about Henry. He was one of life's losers.

But there was a single ray of hope in his case: his alleged victim had also been a Negro.

Just as Henry's last name didn't matter, a cornerstone of the paternalistic tradition of the South is the forgiveness of Negroes for crimes against members of their own race. Although responsible Negroes oppose the practice, they can do little about it unless they happen to be one of those few who intermittently survive the selection system to sit as a member of a jury. I was told that in the event Henry's case ever reached the jury stage and any Negro remained on the venire, if the state didn't strike him I should.

"One Negro on a jury with eleven white men would vote to send your man to the electric chair," an older lawyer advised. "A white jury in Birmingham won't punish a Negro for a crime against Negroes the same way they might punish whites."

In principle, I could see the evils of the system, although I of course approved its immediate application in this case.

I finally met with Henry in the county jail on the ninth floor of the courthouse. First through the sheriff's office, then past a double-locked door, then up a small elevator run by a Negro short-term trusty, then through double-locked doors to the warden's office. There I signed in and was escorted by a deputy to the capital offense block. In a small, narrow room with one table, two chairs, and a barred window, I confronted my client.

To the usual barrier blocking communication between client and appointed attorney—the distrust of the Negro for a strange white man—in Henry's case there were added complications. He could neither read nor write, and what I had mistaken in the courtroom for fear proved to be an advanced respiratory and heart ailment. Henry could hardly talk, gasping and swallowing with every word. A painful first interview drew from him the name of his physician. Nothing else.

It was clear that if I were to get any information concerning the circumstances of Henry's alleged crime I would have to visit the scene myself and talk to witnesses in the area. Together with George Briggs, another young lawyer who had recently begun practice, I traveled across town on a pleasant Saturday afternoon into a Birmingham Negro neighborhood off Georgia Road. We parked the car and got out to walk around the dirt alley where the alleged crime took place. George said he had a feeling of being watched from windows opaque with dirt in the nearby alley shacks. We walked across the street and knocked on the front of a duplex shotgun house. The door was open, and after a long wait we decided to walk in.

There, in a rear room, on a filthy, unkempt bed made up of torn and patched rags and blankets we finally found a Negro woman nursing a baby. Flies crawled on her breast. At least eight other people were crowded into that small room.

"Whatchawan'?" muttered a voice from the far side. I told them that I represented Henry and asked for a witness by name.

"Got the wrong house," replied the woman on the bed. "Ain' nobody that name heah."

I asked if anybody else had witnessed the incident across the street involving my client and the deceased.

"Ain' seen nothin'," replied several voices from various parts of the room.

Saturday is no day to spend in a Negro slum area in Birmingham—but on any day, we were to learn, slum-dwelling Negroes tell nothing about anything—what or whom they have seen or know. Lawyers, bill collectors and police all get the same treatment: "N'a such" or "Doan' live heah" or "Ain' seen nothin'." Generations of experience have taught the Negro slum dweller not to help white men looking for Negroes.

George and I left the duplex and walked back across the street to the scene of the crime. The alley, between two rows of grimy houses set up on stilts, was all hardpacked earth and dust. Even in the cool autumn I felt hot, knowing how oppressive the area must have been during Birmingham's steaming summer months. We picked our way among pieces of jagged metal and glass where barefoot little Negro children were playing.

George looked at me and shook his head. Up to that point, we had both spent our lives passing neighborhoods and alleyways like this. Occasionally we had glimpsed them when we had waited as children in the car while Mother picked up the Negro maid. Now we were grown men, looking for a shred of evidence and justice in a dusty, fly-infested alley, face to face with the other side of our own lives that we had never known existed.

We returned to the car and drove away. In a few minutes we were back in civilization. Only then did George break the silence.

"Jesus Christ," he said. "Jesus Christ."

Henry died in jail of natural causes. But, before he died, investigation of the circumstances surrounding his crime had taught a young lawyer never again to judge a client's case by first impression.

According to testimony finally extracted from Henry's neighbors, the paralytic widow woman of the coroner's description had somehow managed, three days before her violent death, to catch him asleep and kick him into insensibility. She was no stranger to the defendant, for they had in fact been living together for months. Then, at the fateful noon hour, she had stood among a crowd of neighbors, her arm around another man, and taunted Henry.

"She say, 'He ain't no good as a man no mo',' " a witness told me. And with the cackle of laughter in his ears Henry stopped, picked up a gun barrel lying on the ground, and swung. In that elemental world in which he was dying, Henry, who couldn't work, or read, or write, or even talk, had been revealed to all as being impotent. And so he killed her.

Henry had lost his struggle against the existing order. On a plea of guilty he had been sentenced to live his few remaining days in jail and in the end I was powerless to help him, a victim of violence pent up within himself.

I was learning something about the ordered society I had grown up in. After only a year of the practice of law in Birmingham, I had seen that for some there was no peace in our valley. There never really had been.

V

Politics: The Button-Down Bloody Shirt

THE MAGIC CITY sign in front of the Terminal Station had rusted and tarnished. It was removed like a wreath turned brown in a graveyard. Birmingham and Alabama had suddenly been thrust into a destructive new era, and it seemed that even the symbols of past hope were to disappear from sight.

It was 1958 and three years had passed since the Lucy riots, together with the Montgomery bus boycott, had triggered the first explosions of the long night of race violence. The Ku Klux Klan was back, if not respectable then at least more active than it had been in twenty years. The increasingly militant Negro citizens of Birmingham had a new integration leader, the Rev. Fred L. Shuttlesworth. A widening spectrum of violence carried from the absurd—a group of white toughs slugging Nat King Cole on stage at the auditorium—to the unspeakable—the castration of a Negro man whose life's misfortune it was to be standing by the wrong road at the wrong time.

The city was shocked by the crime. White men were arrested, tried and given maximum legal sentences for mayhem. The charge could have been murder, according to medical opinion, except that by pouring turpentine on their victim's wound the accused unwittingly, for their own twisted purposes, saved his life.

Birmingham was being whiplashed between the militance of Shuttlesworth and the increasing frenzy of the white supremacists. Inevitably Eugene "Bull" Connor, who had earned a reputation for "knowing how to handle agitators," was returned to office in 1957. By a slim margin Connor defeated Robert Lindbergh, a well-meaning former sheriff's deputy who had been unable to curb the racial restlessness of the city. Under Birmingham's three-man commission form of government, Connor now commanded the police and fire departments. He was also responsible for the community's educational system. If confronted with law set forth by the Supreme Court in the Brown case, Birmingham's newly-elected educational head could be counted on simply to repeat his legendary statement of years before: "We're not goin' to have white folks and nigras segregatin' together in this man's town."

The state too had been undergoing a political metamorphosis. The Boutwell school placement law had been passed by the legislature, establishing standards to be used in transferring children from one school to another. First in Alabama, then in other Southern states, the school placement procedure was to be adopted and utilized in the struggle against desegregation. Race was not a factor mentioned in the law, but, first for outright resistance, then later for token compliance the placement act was to become an important weapon in segregation's arsenal. There was talk of closing the schools if integration came. A movement was under way to abolish Macon County before increased voter registration permitted Negroes to take power. George Wallace had long since broken with outgoing Governor Folsom and had begun his own campaign for the Mansion. He had threatened to jail FBI "snoopers" checking voter registration documents in his circuit.

And, on a personal level, there was a great change in my legal career. I had left the corporate law firm to open my own office. With a little money saved, some second-hand furniture and a partner equally possessed of audacity of spirit and paucity of assets, I made the plunge.

The young lawyer who hangs out a lone shingle or goes into partnership with a friend is the freest of men, shackled only by his economic status—and his wife's shorthand. Camille and my partner's wife shared the office's secretarial duties our first year. Time, of which there was far too much available those early months, would determine the nature and the limitations of a growing practice. Meanwhile I stepped up my community affairs activities and waited for the "big case," comforted by the thought that whatever we were building now would be our own.

In early spring of 1958 the gubernatorial primary campaign to choose Big Jim Folsom's successor got under way. Fourteen candidates and ten hillbilly bands traveled the state in what *Life* magazine called "an electiontime spectacular." But this governor's race was to be far different from any which had gone before. One issue, *the* issue, dominated the field. There were all the old showmanship, the crowds, the promises of bigger and better pensions, wider and smoother roads, cleaner and purer government—and segregation. And segregation. And segregation.

Four years after the Supreme Court of the United States had ruled that no state could segregate its school system by races, not one candidate's voice was raised in the Alabama gubernatorial primary—not one of fourteen—to prepare the people of our state for compliance with law. From television, from the rostrum, from buckboards and from the stump, the thesis was stated, repeated, shouted: "I will maintain segregation of the races." . . . "We will preserve our Southern way of life." . . . "There will be no integration of the public schools of Alabama."

The race finally settled among three top leaders: State Senator James H. Faulkner, Attorney General John Patterson and Judge Wallace.

Faulkner at first tried to emulate Folsom's progressive approach, but switched emphasis as the campaign stepped up and his opponents' hard segregationist line took hold. A quiet-spoken man, he ended by promising to go to jail if necessary to preserve segregation.

Patterson had become attorney general after his father, who had been elected to the job in 1954, was assassinated on a street in his home town of Phenix City. He had led the charge against vice and corruption in Phenix City, but by record and public utterance he emerged as the campaign's most intransigent opponent of what he called "race mixing." As attorney general, Patterson had filed suit to outlaw the NAACP in Alabama.

Wallace had come full circle since his days as a Folsom campaign lieutenant in 1954. Now, four years later, his campaign featured Confederate flags, rebel yells, and the endorsement of many of the very interests he and Folsom had opposed four years before. The Little Judge was a gifted politician.

A myth has grown up that in the 1958 run-off between Patterson and Wallace—Faulkner had run a weak third—the judge took a "liberal" position. In fact, Wallace, having been outflanked on the right by his opponent, had seized an opportunity to brand Patterson with the brush of Ku Klux Klan support. However, the move was simply tactical and Wallace was then, as in his successful campaign of 1962, a vocal advocate of resistance to desegregation orders.

On run-off election day I could not bring myself to vote for either candidate. The state's political dialogue had been reduced to gibberish, and between two candidates both pledged unequivocally to resist or circumvent the law of the land I saw no real democratic, no "lesser-of-evils" choice. The responsible people of Alabama—our business interests, our civic leaders, organized labor, our educators, our communications media, our clergy and public officials themselves—had permitted the democratic process of our state to disintegrate into raucous and dangerous demagoguery. Not a "moderate" voice was raised, not a "moderate" hand lifted, not a "moderate" protest uttered as candidates for the highest office in Alabama campaigned from the Tennessee Valley to the Gulf of Mexico, shouting defiance of law and court orders.

Patterson was elected and Wallace went to Mongomery to take up the practice of law and renew his quest for higher office. The voters of Alabama had made their choice. It had been a choice, I knew, not of candidates, but of weapons.

Fly the Banners of Confidence:
Tell 100 persons today this fact about our City—Birmingham's residential suburbs are often called the most beautiful residential sections in America!

So boasts the Birmingham *News*.

"Over the mountain" in Birmingham describes a social syndrome common among cities in this country. New York has its Westchester, San Francisco its Nob Hill, Atlanta its Buckhead—all represent, in varying degrees, the classic American social goal of "the right side of the tracks." The right side of the tracks in Birmingham is the south side of the mountain. The city proper rests in Jones Valley, flanked on the south by Red Mountain. Beyond Red Mountain—and beyond the steaming asphalt and steel mill heat—is Shades Valley, the dale of money, power, influence, security and, above all, comfort. All things in Shades Valley and its two chief communities, Homewood and Mountain Brook, where I lived, are built for comfort, and if all its inhabitants are not fabulously wealthy, as envious steel mill workers imagine, they are certainly comfortable. Their homes, with spacious lawns and yards, are comfortable. Their friendly, personal relationships with other members of their community—from mayor to traffic officer to corner druggist to the next-door neighbor—are comfortable. This is the comfort of the suburban South, the simple pleasures of small-town living made even more pleasant by the imported creature comforts of the affluent society. It is the comfort of church socials, along with two cars to the family and private country day schools for the kids; of the social ideals of the Old South pleasantly spiced with an occasional flying visit to bask in the Bahamas or to shop on Fifth Avenue, New York. In brief, a comfort which, in an industrial metropolis that earns its keep on hot steel and slag, only money can buy.

Homewood and Mountain Brook, like most satellite communities, are insulated from the conflicts and problems of the central city. That, after all, is one reason for moving "over the mountain." The insulation of the suburban life is not simply geographical or social, however. North and South, the flight away from the city and its problems involves a degree of political and moral detachment as well. In the Birmingham area, this detachment of the "better people"—those with affluence, education and the potential for leadership—compounded the central city's dilemma.

Relatively few Negroes live in Homewood, none in Mountain Brook—and that, too, is a motivation for moving "over the mountain," just as it is for Northern and Eastern suburbanites. This issue was to be a decisive one in the Birmingham suburban merger campaign of 1959.

By spring, 1959, our law practice had survived its first, perilous year. Things were looking up. If clients were not yet knocking down our doors, neither were creditors.

Camille's father had given Charles a beagle puppy for Christmas and with Jewel as our excuse we joined the house hunters. A small white house with green shutters in Mountain Brook caught Camille's heart and so we moved.

We were to learn to love this house which, as objects often

do, was to merge in memory with events. One year from now Charles was to walk the one block from our door to his first-grade classroom at Crestline School. He and his friends Bobby and Bruce and Billy and Steve and Scott and Gary and Chris and all the others were to play ball in the yard or down the street. And Jewel was to ignore the doghouse to sleep at the foot of Charles' bed.

The neighborhood was perfect. Unlike many of today's suburban developments it had inhabitants ranging in age from the very young to the retired. And they were friendly. There were no quarrels over dogs and cats, children or lot lines.

Our church, St. Luke's Episcopal, was not more than two blocks away, and we were a fifteen-minute drive from the office.

In this home Camille and I were to entertain our friends, watch our son learn and plan and grow and look forward to life in Birmingham.

Two years would pass before we installed the floodlights.

Word came to me that certain of the city's "Big Mules"— Jim Folsom's term to describe the moneyed powers of Birmingham—were discussing the possibility of an all-out drive to merge the suburbs into the central city. Similar campaigns had been defeated in former years, but the list of names associated with the proposed campaign was impressive. And the city's two newspapers, the morning *Post-Herald*, a Scripps-Howard publication, and the evening *News*, owned by the Newhouse chain, were getting ready to put their editorial weight behind the drive. For once, it seemed to me, Birmingham was waking up to the need for change and progress. For the first time in my memory, community leaders were speaking openly in terms of what the city needed, not what it had. Criticism was being heard—an unusual civic phenomenon in Birmingham.

My hopes rose. Things had gotten worse—now they might get better. I pondered what had triggered the merger movement, and concluded that the city had deteriorated to a degree that even the most myopic of our community leaders could not ignore. But, whatever the motives behind the new merger campaign, I saw in it the long-awaited opportunity that younger members of the community had been hoping for. Once the leadership resources of the over-the-mountain communities had been brought into Birmingham, a breakthrough could be made on the city's festering problems. Some who were for merger simply wanted the white suburbanites to vote in the central city's elections to offset the feared but not yet registered Negro population. But, in concrete terms, I considered only that with Homewood and Mountain Brook citizens voting in Birmingham municipal elections, Bull Connor's small popular majority would be erased. Merger would be a big step forward for a city that had stood still too long.

I planned to help as much as my law practice would permit in making the merger campaign a success. Then a telephone call from a friend and fellow attorney, George Peach Taylor, let me know that the campaign's planners— a group that included former governor Frank Dixon, former mayor Cooper Green, former state senator James A. Simpson and other powerful political, business and economic leaders —were considering me for a key role in what would be a pivotal election in our city's history. I was flattered. With the older heads behind us and the younger men spearheading the effort, I felt sure we could win. Who said Birmingham was a dying city?

Peach was a resident of Homewood. I lived in Mountain Brook. We were to pool our energies in convincing the voters of the two over-the-mountain suburbs of the virtues of merger. In order to win, we had to gain a majority of "yes" votes in each of the suburban communities. Birmingham's city government had already agreed to take in the two communities if the suburban voters approved.

What was at stake could be seen by studying the recent history of Atlanta, Georgia, 160 miles away. Atlanta too is a Deep Southern city—one far more rooted in the region's history and traditions than upstart Birmingham. Ten years before our merger campaign, Atlanta had annexed its wealthy Buckhead suburb. Mayor Willie B. Hartsfield was then able to depend on Buckhead's participation, leadership and voting power to help steer his city on a progressive course in race relations. Now Birmingham had its chance.

The campaign would not be an easy one, however. Despite powerful local support, merger had its opponents and they were well financed and vocal. We anticipated that their campaign would hinge on the age-old questions of taxation, municipal services and other virtues of decentralized "small town" government. The people of Homewood and Mountain Brook had grown used to the comforts and convenience of their towns. Their communities were relatively well organized—especially Mountain Brook—and, although Mountain Brook had no public parks or municipal swimming pools, such facilities were not really needed in what was essentially a country club community.

Peach and I worked ourselves to the point of exhaustion, carrying both our separate law practices and the brunt of campaign activities into late-night sessions. We argued the case for merger before civic clubs and on television discussion panels. We met regularly with the group of elder city statesmen charting the campaign's course—and, if I learned a great deal watching them operate, I seldom hesitated to speak up and make my own opinions known. It was my first real contest with the people who moved community and state affairs— and I was enjoying every minute of it.

But segregation was again to develop into the make-or-break issue. There was no escaping its pervasive and overriding impact on the consciousness of the electorate, even the "better people," who by education and insulation might be expected to assess the issue in a reasonable light. I had come to believe that education was the key to solving the South's race problem. I was to learn in the spring of 1959 that bigotry and intolerance can lurk behind a sheepskin as well as a hood.

The Parent-Teacher Association of Crestline School in Mountain Brook had called a meeting to consider whether their community should support a separate municipal school system. Speakers addressed a packed auditorium of well-dressed, upper-middle-class mothers and fathers on the subject of school financing, organization and priorities. There had been proposals to close down schools rather than desegregate and the man who carried the evening was a senior member of one of Alabama's oldest, best-established law firms, educated at the finest schools in the East, trained through the years of study and practice in constitutional law. He rose, the voice of authority, and he spoke sincerely and eloquently. His talk resolved into one salient point: if Mountain Brook, which had no Negro families, had a separate municipal school system, an integration case involving the county's or Birmingham's schools would not force Mountain Brook's schools to close. In terms of the merger issue, this meant that, if Mountain Brook's school system remained separate, though Birmingham's schools might close down, the over-the-mountain communities could keep their schools open—and segregated.

The argument took hold, not only at that PTA meeting, but throughout the suburbs. Rather than accept their responsibility to the greater community and work to keep the schools open as citizens of Birmingham, the suburbanites sought to isolate themselves, to take care of their own schools regardless of what happened to the school children of Birmingham proper. A Maginot Line could be drawn at the Birmingham city boundary and the onrush of desegregation could be stopped at the corporate limits.

We were beaten. Incredibly, it seemed, Homewood and Mountain Brook voters rejected the merger. I watched the returns in the city hall of Mountain Brook—and concluded that in the ballots of thousands of "better people," the bloody shirt of Alabama race politics had produced its tailor-made, button-down models.

The defeat was to result in a reversal of gears in the attitudes of the community leaders who had put their influence on the line for merger. Once burned they would become even more conservative and timid in their plans to solve the city's problems. And, having been burned by the race issue, they would be especially wary about any proposals that might get them burned again.

"Fly the Banners of Confidence," the Birmingham *News* would implore its community some four years later. "Tell 100 persons today this fact about our City—Birmingham's Mountain Brook—highest income area in the South, ranks eighth in the nation."

That it was not "Birmingham's Mountain Brook" did not seem to faze community leaders after the defeat of 1959. Like every other harsh, unpleasant fact concerning our city—including changes in the world that pounded at our city's ancient racial landmarks—it was much more comfortable to pretend it just didn't exist.

CHAPTER

VI

The Place for an Honest Man Is Jail
(Part 1)

THE POLITICIAN DEALS in multitudes, the lawyer in individuals. By 1960, five years after graduation from the university, I still thought in terms of a political career. But successful politicians, in Alabama as elsewhere, do not by choice associate themselves with unpopular causes. Within a year my participation in cases involving the freedom of two individuals would alter my plans. I began the period as a politician. I ended it as a lawyer.

In Alabama, Democratic Presidential electors are nominated in a spring primary. Electors nominated are listed on the November ballot under the party label. The names of Presidential and Vice-Presidential candidates do not appear, and no law binds electors to cast their electoral college vote for party candidates. In early 1960, a full-fledged movement was under way to prevent the national Democratic party from receiving any Alabama electoral votes.

An "independent" slate of electors, pledged to vote for whomever they pleased in November, was opposed by a "loyalist" slate pledged to support the party's convention nominees. A second Dixiecrat revolt, similar to that in 1948, was in the making. That year Alabama's electors were pledged to vote for J. Strom Thurmond, then governor of South Carolina, for President and Mississippi Governor Fielding Wright for Vice-President. Alabama voters were not given the opportunity to vote for—or, for that matter, against—the President of the United States, Harry S. Truman. His name did not appear on the ballot, nor did the names of any electors pledged to vote for him. In 1960, the discordant issue was once again the national party's civil rights position. The "independents" proposed to defeat any Democratic ticket whose views on the race question were considered "anti-Southern."

I was soon dividing my time between law office and "loyalist" campaign headquarters in downtown Birmingham.

My political duties included party worker organization, as well as television and speaking appearances. The campaign between the two party factions became acrimonious, with the maintenance of segregation the chief issue. This was to be Foots Clement's last political assignment on behalf of the party and the state he loved, and I was in close touch with him as the campaign progressed. It was to be one of his hardest fights, for time was working against his side now, and the old reliable slogans and shibboleths—F.D.R., the New Deal, the call to traditional party colors—were losing their pulling power. The burden of political battle was falling upon the shoulders of a new generation, and it was up to us to keep the party machinery from Dixiecrat control. I was on a political mission—and the last thing I wanted was to become involved in an unpopular civil rights case.

Thomas C. Reeves, a twenty-year-old Phi Beta Kappa pre-ministerial student at Birmingham-Southern College, was arrested by Birmingham police on a Sunday afternoon while assisting in a church outing. The young man had been instrumental in bringing together white students from Birmingham-Southern and Negro students from the city's two Negro colleges, Miles and Daniel Payne, for periodic discussions and exchange of ideas. He had also risen at a meeting to oppose the formation of a pro-segregationist church laymen's organization. He had met with Negro students in a dormitory on the campus of Daniel Payne on the Saturday night before his arrest.

In short, Thomas C. Reeves was an "agitator," by every definition of the community in which he lived. He was jailed. There were demands that he be expelled from school. But Tom Reeves was lucky. In his hour of need he found a powerful friend who ignored his sense of community politics but retained a real sense of academic freedom. Men like that, even in the cloistered world of university life, are hard to find. But Dr. Henry King Stanford was such a man. He was president of Birmingham-Southern College—and he'd be damned if they'd run roughshod over one of his students.

Dr. Stanford sought legal counsel for Reeves. He was

turned down several times, and finally a lawyer suggested he get in touch with me. When I received his call I was deeply involved in political activities. But it occurred to me that if Henry King Stanford, a successful and highly-respected educator, could go out on a limb for a young man who chose to meet with Negroes on a Negro campus in Birmingham, Alabama, perhaps there was more to the art of the possible than politicians dared attempt. Defeating the Dixiecrats was important, but only because it would be a step toward building a community where a young man like Tom Reeves would not be deprived of his freedom of belief. With another young lawyer, I agreed to undertake his defense.

Feeling was high about the case. Previously, a cross had been burned on the college campus as a warning to our client—and to the school's administration. Dr. Stanford stood his ground. Reeves' father, visiting a barber shop near the campus, had heard two men suggest that "they ought to string up that kid at the college," and he wanted his son to withdraw from school. Dr. Stanford would not hear of it. There was alumni pressure. Dr. Stanford would not budge. Newspaper publicity about the case exacerbated community tensions centering about the campus. There were demands, threats, recriminations. But Tom Reeves had found a friend who practiced what he taught. His case was to be continued several times and never tried. In the end, following commencement, the young man was to leave Birmingham for his home in Tennessee with a dismissal of his court case, a degree, and with Phi Beta Kappa honors.

My worry about identification with a case involving

racial issues had been without foundation. It had not been necessary for me to appear in court on Reeves' behalf. And, other than among my friends, who already knew how I felt, no one was to associate me with my client. In the dismissal of the Reeves case I had also won a reprieve for myself. It was to be short-lived. For, by demonstrating a willingness to help Tom Reeves, I had set myself on a course from which it would be difficult to turn back.

The primary contest ended in frustration for both factions. Six "independent" and five "loyalist" electors were chosen. But somehow the Reeves case seemed more important in terms of what direction I should take. I still felt that the art of the possible had its rewards. But, as I began to recognize, watching a strong university president refuse to compromise what he knew to be right, so has the art of the impossible.

"Hello, Montgomery, this is Lyndon B. Johnson, candidate for Vice-President. . . . Vote Democratic."

The exhilaration of a national election had finally come to Alabama. No longer was the state taken for granted. For this opportunity to take part in the mainstream of national political affairs we could give backhanded thanks to the growing Alabama Republican movement. In former Presidential election years, Alabama and other Deep Southern states had been bypassed by members of the national ticket. But now the Republicans were threatening to carry the state and I was on a campaign train loaded with politicians, carrying Senator Johnson and his entourage from the state capital to a television appearance in Birmingham.

[65]

I had been named state chairman of the Kennedy-Johnson speakers committee. My job was to schedule speaking appearances in all parts of the state, either to make speakers available to groups or to fill engagements myself. To the already heated issue of race had been added the fire of religious bigotry.

Thirty-two years before, Senator "Cotton Tom" Heflin had almost defeated the Al Smith ticket in Alabama by telling his rural audiences that if Smith were elected "the Pope will sail up Mobile Bay in a submarine." The story had long been part of the state's humorous political lore, but the joke was forgotten in the autumn of 1960. Now a majority of the voters of Anglo-Saxon Protestant Alabama, even in the rural areas, were too sophisticated to swallow the raw, outlandish religious bigotry of 1928. But religious bigotry there was, virulent and potentially disastrous for the Democratic ticket.

The Johnson whistlestop tour was the high point of the party's campaign effort in the state. For me, it was also the most pleasant assignment in what otherwise had become a vicious and ugly repetition of previous campaigns which turned on the race issue. The issue was a trap, as much a trap for the well meaning as for the aggressive demagogue.

"What has emerged in Alabama," wrote a friend and former college roommate, "is a politics of Segmanship—the strategy of outflanking the political enemy on the race issue without going over the brink of secession."

Vic Gold had practiced law and political public relations in Alabama until 1958, when he moved to Washington. From a distance he followed the course of state elections and wrote warning that "if you mean to move ahead in Alabama politics, or even just to stay put, you will have to get caught up in the Segman's game."

"Segmanship is a demagogic discipline that even old Tom Heflin might need time to master," wrote Gold. "After all, it was one thing for an Alabama leader in the 1920's to rise in the Senate and tell the world that the Negro *should* stay in his place; it is infinitely more complex for today's Alabama politician to convince his constituents (if not himself) that come court order or federal troops, the Negro *will* stay in his place. But that is the Segman's burden: to maintain the illusion that despite what is happening, nothing will happen —unless, of course, the opposition is elected."

A few days after receiving my former roommate's letter, I was debating a Republican spokesman at the Bessemer High School. Once again, as in past campaigns, I was on the defensive, explaining that the national Democratic party record on civil rights was not really any more "anti-Southern" than the Republican record. Finally, after twenty minutes of bearing the brunt of opposition jibes, my patience ended. "Say what you will," I snapped, pointing an accusing finger toward my Republican opponent. "It wasn't the Democrats in Little Rock who carried bayonets."

The crowd cheered. But no sooner had the words been spoken than I realized the awful cost of my debating point. The issue was a trap. Every white man in Alabama was caught up in it.

VII

The Place for an Honest Man Is Jail
(Part 2)

"EVERY CHANNEL OF COMMUNICATION, every medium of mutual interest, every reasoned approach, every
inch of middle ground has been fragmented by the emotional
dynamite of racism. . . ."

So wrote Harrison Salisbury of Birmingham's racial tensions in April, 1960. Salisbury had come to the city to report
news, but his two-part *New York Times* series itself became
one of the most newsworthy events in Birmingham's history.
Local criticism of the handling of the city's racial affairs had
been almost nonexistent. But in this case the "outsider"
Times was critical. Eventually, every medium of communication—the three major television networks, Northern and
Eastern newspapers and magazines, the foreign press—all
would be accused by community leaders of "distorting our

city's image." And even local media would feel the sting of rebuke at such times as their reportage of racial matters, in the opinion of some, did not serve to enhance Birmingham's "image."

Neither of Birmingham's two newspapers, the morning *Post-Herald* and the evening *News,* had been critical of their city's approach to racial problems. The *Post-Herald* was as hard-line segregationist as respectable journalism allows. The *News* was more realistic and attempted to face community problems in a less die-hard fashion. But, over all, the community pattern of editorial comment ran a zigzag course of leadership in racial matters. The editorial pages called for law and order one day, and attacked the Supreme Court's 1954 school decision—the law of the land—the next.

In the Salisbury case, the local press and not the "rabid" element it so often deplores catalyzed an explosion in community resentment which was to keep the racial waters roiled for a long time to come. The *News* and *Post-Herald* both ran the Salisbury articles under headlines best described as skeptical, then followed up with bitter editorial-page denunciations of the *Times,* Salisbury and that Pulitzer Prize winner's reporting. City officials demanded a retraction. When the *Times* agreed to publish a statement by two community business leaders, Birmingham's newspaper executives were consulted in preparation of the article. But following its publication by the *Times,* the *Post-Herald* still was not satisfied and editorially rebuked what it called the weakness of the rebuttal.

Although the *Times* had made space available for an answer from Birmingham, it did not print a retraction of the Salisbury articles. With community indignation at fever pitch, city officials filed suit for defamation. A local jury was to determine whether the *New York Times* and Harrison E. Salisbury had libeled their community and its leaders.

Salisbury had written of the failure of channels of communication between the races.

"No New Yorker can readily measure the climate of Birmingham today," his April 8, 1960, *Times* article reported. "Whites and blacks still walk the same streets. But the streets, the water supply and the sewer system are about the only public facilities they share. Ball parks and taxicabs are segregated. So are libraries. . . . A drive is on to forbid Negro music on white radio stations. . . .

"Every channel of communication, every medium of mutual interest, every reasoned approach, every inch of middle ground has been fragmented by the emotional dynamite of racism. . . ." Whether or not the *Times* had been correct in its facts or conclusions, the Salisbury articles deeply shocked the city. This was not the Birmingham most of the community's white leaders knew; not the city they loved. They felt wronged and aggrieved.

If the breakdown in interracial communications of which Salisbury wrote had occurred, it had not always existed. More than 30 percent of Birmingham's population is Negro. Prior to the mid-1950's, unofficial biracial committees dealing with specific community race matters had functioned in the city. But, as racial tensions mounted, biracial committees were disbanded. Hard-line segregationists opposed any biracial discussion of community affairs and even the term "mod-crate" came to have opprobrious connotations. At one time, a United Appeal Fund drive was threatened with a boycott by some because word spread that a biracial group was a fund recipient. Biracial organization work was a socially risky business.

Nevertheless, one group that continued to operate in this vital area was the Alabama Council on Human Relations, an affiliate of the Southern Regional Council. The council served to maintain communications between the white and Negro communities and to gather and disseminate information about racial problems. As a result, council leaders, like the Reverend Robert E. Hughes, understood the community's race problem in a way that most Birminghamians could never know it.

Reverend Hughes had been allowed to accept assignment to the executive directorship of the council by Bishop Clare Purcell of the North Alabama Methodist Conference. A soft-spoken, slightly-built young minister who had been kept from missionary work in Africa by an ulcer, Hughes was a knowledgeable contact point for out-of-town newsmen who often found official information channels closed to them. Predictably, he was victimized by local smear-sheet artists, late-night telephone callers and other merchants of hate. A cross was burned on his front lawn. His wife was subjected to taunts and threats. Opposing the pro-segregation laymen's organization, he even ran into trouble with his fellow churchmen. Still, Bob Hughes carried on what he believed to be his assigned mission. Although a man not impervious to human stress or mortal fear—as his ulcer seemed to indicate —he was a Christian minister, a white Christian minister in the Deep South, and he sought to live in the teachings of his faith. As the Salisbury episode unfolded, Bob Hughes would be driven to pay a high price for his Christian principles in an area that boasts the "City of Churches."

In Alabama, the sources of news are privileged and no reporter may be compelled to give the names of persons from whom he has received information in preparation of an article. Reporter Salisbury's modus operandi during his Birmingham visit was soon the subject of intense scrutiny.

First, the telephone numbers of Salisbury's outgoing calls from the hotel at which he had stayed during his visit were obtained. The New York reporter had used his room telephone and hotel switchboard to call his news sources. Hughes' telephone number apparently was one of those listed.

Then, in Bessemer, Alabama, ten miles down the road from Birmingham, in Jefferson County, a grand jury was to consider whether their community also had been defamed by the Salisbury articles. Bessemer is a pocket-sized version of Birmingham, a grim-looking industrial town that has one of the highest percentages of nonwhite population in the nation for a community its size. The town had been started by one of the area's early promoters, Henry DeBardeleben, who bought up a portion of the New Orleans Cotton Exposition and moved it to his town site. The Jamaica building had become part of a rolling mill. The Montezuma building had become a hotel.

The Bessemer grand jury, certain to determine whether Alabama's criminal libel laws had been violated in the Salisbury series, had a subpoena duces tecum served on

Reverend Hughes to appear before it on September 1, 1960. A subpoena merely requires the witness to be present. A subpoena duces tecum requires him not only to be present but also to bring with him requested documents. Hughes' subpoena duces tecum required him to bring "all records, books, cancelled checks, memorandums, letters, correspondence showing all contributions and donations made to Robert E. Hughes, or the Alabama Council on Human Relations, during the period from January 1, 1958, to the present date; all records showing who made said contributions or donations; all records showing all expenditures of the Alabama Council on Human Relations for said period and then and there to testify . . ."

Although Reverend Hughes had no compunction about testifying to the grand jury, he felt that the order for lists and organization records made the council the real investigative target. The white membership of the council ranged from businessmen to fellow Methodist ministers, from established attorneys to the wives of prominent citizens. Exposure of their names and the names of contributors could subject all to harassment such as he had suffered.

If Hughes complied with the subpoena to produce records, he would in all probability be off the hook of grand jury investigation himself. But compliance could jeopardize individual careers of members and contributors, as well as destroy the effectiveness of the last remaining biracial organization in Alabama. He communed with his conscience and made his decision. He would resist the grand jury order. He would fight the authority of the subpoena duces tecum through the courts.

Bob Hughes needed a lawyer. And it was common knowledge in Birmingham that even the powerful and wealthy *New York Times* had had difficulty procuring counsel in its libel cases. Hughes conferred with council members and finally sought help from one of the city's larger firms. There was no help for him there. He was in the maelstrom of controversy. The respected and, incidentally, safe firm could render him no assistance.

The then president of the Junior Bar telephoned me. Other Bar officials were in Washington, D.C., at the annual meeting of the American Bar Association. I had planned to attend. The conversation ended with the Junior Bar president's telling me that he would issue a statement that he, as an official of the Bar, had asked me to undertake Hughes' defense.

I wasn't a member of the council and I knew Hughes only casually. The law firm which had last refused the case could afford its stigma better than I could. And, after all, this same firm had referred Dr. Stanford to me in the Reeves case. Once a year was enough. It seemed to be their turn now. But I agreed to talk with Hughes: someone had to.

Within hours of Reverend Hughes' decision, I was faced with its consequences. Once again, as with the Reeves case, I had to consider what effect handling a controversial race relations case might have on my own career. There were possible economic consequences—and our practice was beginning to grow. And there were bound to be political consequences far greater even than those of the Reeves case. Before taking the case up with my law partner, Jim Shores, I knew I had to discuss these matters with Camille. She, too, had an investment in our practice, beyond the interest that most women have in their husbands' careers. Camille had persevered through my hectic law school days, pacifying our infant son so that I could study late nights in our crowded university quarters. She had lent encouragement, not to mention long secretarial hours, when I decided to leave the corporate firm and strike out on my own. And she had patiently abided my periodic detours from a law office with paying clients to political hustings with nonpaying candidates and causes. Now, with the Hughes case, we might be risking all this investment in time and toil; and possibly more, for representing Hughes meant front-line involvement on the unpopular side of a bitter community controversy. There was the possibility of unpleasant social and personal ramifications, a consideration that no family with a child in school can wholly ignore. And lurking in the background was the greater unpleasantness of having our telephone number added to the hatemongers' list for nighttime calls.

I explained all this to Camille but there was really no need. Along with Jim, she believed that we really had no choice in the matter. I called Reverend Hughes and informed him that he had a legal counsel, for better or worse.

By nightfall Reverend Hughes' friends were mobilizing. Father Albert S. Foley, a Jesuit priest who taught at Springhill College in Mobile, traveled to Birmingham and as president of the council undertook the job of raising funds for Hughes' defense fund.

Time was short. Hughes' subpoena duces tecum ordered him to appear in court with the council records within forty-eight hours. Research began immediately, and through the night Hughes sat in our office sipping milk while his legal defense—a motion to quash the subpoena duces tecum—was drafted, discarded, redrafted. Legal precedents were hunted down and pinpointed amid a clutter of law books and papers. In the Daisy Bates case in Arkansas, the Supreme Court of the United States had held that the National Association for the Advancement of Colored People did not have to surrender lists of its members to state authorities. A similar ruling applied to John Patterson's attempt, as attorney general, to obtain a court order for NAACP records in Alabama. If that was the law for the NAACP, we felt that should be the law for Hughes and the council. But there was a Birmingham case involving a grand jury's right to order in Ku Klux Klan records—a precedent which I would find useful in one memorable debate outside the courtroom.

Finally, as the first flicker of gray morning light settled upon the valley, Reverend Hughes' legal weapon took shape. Our motion would raise the constitutional defenses provided in the Bill of Rights: freedom of press, speech, worship, assembly and religion. When finally our exhausted secretary finished typing the last word on the last page we all went downstairs into the bracing dawn air and walked across Twenty-first Street toward home, a nap and breakfast. I felt good, the rewarding feeling of exultation and relief that any lawyer experiences when he has worked long hours and done his best to prepare his case. The courtroom drama—the part that the public sees and reads about—was still ahead, only a few hours away. But we were ready, as ready as we could be.

"What do you think will happen?" Bob Hughes asked as we later prepared to leave for the Bessemer courthouse.

"That's for the court and the Lord to decide, Bob," I answered. "I'll do my best in court. The Lord is your jurisdiction."

Our motion to quash was filed and set to be heard before Circuit Judge Gardner F. Goodwyn, Jr., at 11 A.M. At 4 P.M. Judge Goodwyn made his ruling. Motion denied. Hughes was scheduled to testify the following morning and we asked for a one-day delay in order to take an appeal to the Alabama Supreme Court in Montgomery. Request denied.

Immediately, Jim Shores called the clerk of the State Supreme Court. A hearing was set before the high tribunal at 8 A.M. the next morning—one short hour before our client was under orders to appear and produce records in Bessemer. Another all-night work session, with only brief snatches of sleep, lay ahead.

Next morning Jim was arguing before the high court in Montgomery when Hughes and I got into his battered old Chevrolet and headed down the Bessemer highway once again. Before arriving at the courthouse we called Montgomery for word on the Supreme Court's decision. Petition denied. We proceeded to the Bessemer courthouse and into the center of the storm.

Hughes had warned me that the Klan might have representatives near and about the courthouse area. Walking up the courthouse steps, I was not unmindful of the fact that Bessemer was the place where a defendant in a civil rights case had been beaten outside a courtroom. I determined that this was not going to happen to any client of mine. We entered the courthouse and began what was to be an all-day wait. The grand jury was hearing testimony of other witnesses. The hallway outside the grand jury room was crowded and noisy. Other waiting witnesses—lawyers, rabbis, newsmen, businessmen, all subpoenaed to testify in the Salisbury case—were milling about the area. And then my attention was drawn to another group that was there with leaflets—printed diatribes which called my client a "nigger lover."

I stopped for a moment to watch the obvious leader of this group, a tall, ruddy-faced man with zealot eyes and a handful of hate literature. There in the hallowed halls of justice, not far from a room where a grand jury was assembled to consider offenses against the peace and dignity of the State of Alabama, I came face to face with the real thing— not the business-suited, button-down, socially respectable defenders of the status quo, but their unwanted allies, the men of impassioned hatred and incipient violence never far from the surface. There they were, not anonymous voices on a telephone, but out in the open, ready to carry on their own warped form of missionary work. Bob Hughes would spend the following night in jail, but these men were now there to pass out their hate literature in the courthouse corridor.

I walked over to the ruddy-faced tall one, took a leaflet and read it. Then I handed it back.

"I think you and your friends ought to leave," I said. "You're really not doing much good here."

He blinked, muttered something about talking to the "head man" and moved across the hall to whisper to a short, squint-eyed man in a soiled white shirt. To my surprise, this one turned out to be the leader. He and the tall one returned. "You wanna see me, lawyer?" he asked. He did not look at Hughes standing near by, although he must have known his identity. I repeated my request that he and his group leave the area.

Stamping out a cigarette on the courthouse floor he said: "Why should we, lawyer? You can't make us."

Eleven years before, an area Klan leader had been sentenced to nearly two months in jail for refusing to deliver a KKK membership list to a Birmingham circuit court. I had recalled the case and we checked it out in our research. This would now serve as the trump card in my extra-legal debate with the Klan.

"You remember the Morris case?" I asked, referring to the once jailed Klan Kleagle. "If a grand jury is entitled to a membership list from Reverend Hughes, what about its right to Klan records? You and Hughes are in the same boat, whether you like it or not. Have you ever thought about that?"

He uttered a single unprintable word, spat on the court-house floor, turned and walked back to his group. There was an animated conference, and then, to my surprise—for, despite my trump, I really believed such men were impossible to reach—they gathered up their literature and left.

This was to be the high point of our day of waiting. Meanwhile, in Washington, Sigmund Timberg, our associate attorney, was filing a motion with the Supreme Court of the United States seeking a stay of the subpoena duces tecum. The delay in Bessemer was to give us another night for preparation of our case, interspersed with long-distance conferences with Washington counsel.

The next morning, September 2, Reverend Hughes was called to testify. He walked into the grand jury room alone and empty-handed. Attorneys are not permitted to accompany clients who are testifying before a grand jury. Standing in the outer hallway I was gripped by a feeling of helpless frustration. Within minutes, however, the grand jury door opened and the jurors, led by a representative of the solicitor's office, began coming out. (In Alabama, state and county prosecuting attorneys are called solicitors in the old English style.) Bob Hughes was also in tow, and I locked step with him as the crowd moved down the hall toward the courtroom.

Judge Goodwyn was informed that the witness had failed to testify as ordered by the subpoena. I told the court that although he would answer grand jury questions concerning his conversations with Harrison Salisbury, he would not agree to furnish information regarding the council. The judge sent the grand jury members and their reluctant witness back for one more try. It was shortlived. Five minutes later an angry group of jurors was back in the courtroom advising the judge that the witness had again refused to answer questions. Judge Goodwyn asked Hughes if he had indeed refused to comply with grand jury orders.

"Yes, sir," Hughes replied.

"All right, you leave me no alternative," said Judge Goodwyn, "except to adjudge you in contempt of court and order your confinement until you purge yourself of contempt." The judge nodded toward the bailiff. "Confine the witness," he said.

And, in a flurry of activity, Reverend Robert E. Hughes was taken from the crowded courtroom and sent to jail. A short while later I arrived at the jail bringing a measure of reassurance, a bottle of milk for his ulcer—and a copy of *Profiles in Courage.*

At first I was worried about my client's treatment in jail, but surprise, sometimes pleasant and other times unpleasant, is the common denominator of most legal transactions. A lawyer who handles cases involving flesh-and-blood people soon comes to appreciate the total unpredictability of the human elements with which he deals. Bob Hughes, coming into the courthouse, was a target for community contempt, even outrage. Now the same Bob Hughes, jailed, was treated with care and consideration. Not only were court officials and his jailers solicitous about his welfare, but he proceeded to get along famously with his fellow inmates.

That night telephone calls came to my office and to courthouse officials—but this time the calls were neither anonymous nor threatening. Coming primarily from white members of the community, the calls continued during the next day. Many of the callers were ministers. Others were people who wanted to express concern for "a preacher who is just standing up for his rights."

What percentage of the population these callers represented it was impossible to know. But it was certain that there was no widespread public acclaim for the jailing of a Methodist minister—even an integrationist in Jefferson County, Alabama.

One long-distance call did not conform to this pattern, however. It came from the husband of a close relative of Hughes who lived in the Midwest.

"Mr. Morgan, I just read in the newspaper here that Bob Hughes is in jail," he said. "Is that correct?"

"Yes, he is," I replied. "We're doing everything we can to get him out."

"What's he in for?"

"He won't give up some names and information about members of his organization," I explained.

The voice on the other end was suddenly shrill. "Well, tell him to give it to them!"

I allowed, as calmly as was possible, that it wasn't my place to advise a client, especially a man of the cloth, to do something he believed to be wrong. "It's a matter of principle," I concluded.

"Damn it!" came the thundering Midwestern response. *"Tell him to forget his principles!"*

Hughes spent a long Labor Day weekend in jail, but by Tuesday we felt that a Supreme Court ruling on our motion to stay the Bessemer subpoena was imminent. I was visiting my client, advising him of this hopeful possibility, when suddenly his name was called in the jail lobby. He was brought out and handed a piece of paper by the sheriff. It was another subpoena, but this time there was no mention of books, records or lists. And so Bob Hughes went before the Bessemer grand jury, empty-handed.

We had won our point without the necessity of U.S. Supreme Court action. Our petition in Washington was withdrawn, but with the cautious stipulation that "we wish this Court to know of our apprehension, which we sincerely hope will prove groundless, that it may be necessary for us to make a similar application in the future."

But it would not be necessary. The grand jury did not pursue the Hughes matter further.

Salisbury was ultimately indicted by the grand jury on forty-two counts of criminal libel. To date, he has not been served and his indictments are still outstanding. Nor can he return to Alabama without risk of prosecution and imprisonment.

Bob Hughes' secular ordeal had come to an end. Then, as a mocking aftermath, he was brought up on charges before the North Alabama Conference of the Methodist Church in Birmingham. Although the conference had originally approved his work with the Council on Human Relations, a church committee now recommended that he either resign and accept a new assignment or be dismissed from the ministry. By a pro forma vote, without discussion, the committee recommendation was approved. Bob Hughes, who had won his fight for principle in the courts, was about to lose his ministerial rank within his own church. But friendly church officials, knowing Hughes' desire to be a missionary, reached the Methodist bishop in Southern Rhodesia. Reverend Hughes' missionary services were needed in Africa, wired the bishop. Two days later the conference restored Bob Hughes to full rank as a Methodist minister and authorized his transfer to Southern Rhodesia.

The impact of my experiences in the Reeves and Hughes cases fundamentally changed my perspective on the community I called home and toward my role as a Birmingham attorney. I had given up the luxury of detachment from the causes I represented. In political campaigns, submerged in the ebb and flow of organization and people, I had always managed to maintain some degree of personal detachment. Now I myself had become *involved*, not simply as a lawyer but as a member of the community—as a person who had a share of responsibility for the things that were happening to my home and to my client.

Now the late night calls, the anonymous threats, the vicious taunts were to come to my house, aimed at me and at my family. The ring of the telephone in the early-morning hours can be jarring. I would start out of my sleep and head for the kitchen.

"Hello," I'd answer.

"How come you'd represent that nigger lover Hughes?" a voice would ask.

And then before I could answer there was the click of a receiver and the buzzing of a dead line.

"I hear you're a tough son-of-a-bitch," another caller would bark.

"You better watch out, tough guy. Some night we'll get you alone."

But more often than not the sound of heavy breathing would come from the other end of the line, nothing else. Then a click and buzzing silence. Again, just before dawn, another call would come to welcome me back into the world of people who seemed to work all night.

At first, I found it hard to comprehend how my activities and those of a Bob Hughes could be placed in the same category. After all, my representation of a man has nothing to do with his beliefs. In taking the Reeves and Hughes cases, I was only performing my job as an attorney. But then it occurred to me that performance of his job as he saw its responsibilities was really all that put Bob Hughes in the front lines of community controversy. There was no evading the truth of the matter: Bob Hughes and I—much as I had advised that sullen zealot in the Bessemer courthouse corridor—were in the same boat, whether I liked it or not.

"I remember so well driving home alone the afternoon I was removed from the ministry," Bob later wrote me from his post in Southern Rhodesia. "Passing through the South-side Negro area I passed a small Negro boy, eight or nine years old, walking along the gutter kicking a tin can aimlessly. I caught a glimpse of his dejected face in the gathering dusk and the thought struck me that what I had done might have, by a small degree, made his future brighter. For some reason, I suddenly realized that the opposition didn't really matter—the acceptance or rejection of others was not nearly as important as whether or not I had done my best.

"Certainly," he concluded, "we are called upon to be faithful before we're called upon to be effective."

So wrote my client and friend, Bob Hughes, at the end of his journey, about a crucial turning point in my own.

VIII

The Freedom Bus Struck a Pedestrian

THE YOUNG CANDIDATE left the City Hall office where he had just met with Birmingham Police Commissioner T. Eugene "Bull" Connor. He had tried unsuccessfully to insure the commissioner's neutrality in the mayoralty run-off of May, 1961. He took the elevator downstairs and left the building. Outside, the area was strangely empty of people. Suddenly a voice called out: "Mr. King . . . you're Tom King, aren't you?"

Tom King swung around and with the instinctive reflex action of a politician in mid-campaign thrust out his hand as he had done thousands of times in recent weeks. But this would be the most important handshake of the Birmingham mayoralty race of spring, 1961.

"Yes, I'm Tom King," the candidate said, and in an instant his political antennae were signaling danger. His caller was a tall, angular man, ill at ease, who said nothing more but clasped King's hand in a viselike grip. "What do you want?" asked the candidate. Abruptly the man released King's hand, turned and walked rapidly down the street. King stood for a moment; with the strange sixth sense of the politician, he knew he had just been photographed shaking hands with a Negro. He had heard stories of such incidents, but until that moment he did not really believe that anyone was capable of politics on that level. The practical political education of J. Thomas King, thirty-seven-year-old crusader for a better Birmingham, had begun.

Tom King was a native of the Birmingham area, the son of a circuit judge and a young man whose training and talents seemed to point him inevitably toward a position of leadership in his community. At downtown Phillips High School he had been president of the student body. After serving overseas with the Air Force in World War II, he had returned home to attend the university on the G.I. Bill. During these college years he drove a milk truck and held other outside jobs to support his wife and family. A law school graduate, Tom became administrative assistant to Birmingham Congressman George Huddleston, Jr., helping Huddleston handle constituent problems for six years. From this post he came to have first-hand knowledge of community and area needs. A hard-working, no-nonsense person, he was dissatisfied with Birmingham's stagnant economic condition and the city leaders' failure to come to grips with growing community problems. When it became apparent that incumbent Mayor James W. "Jimmie" Morgan would not seek re-election, Tom seemed a natural for the job.

I talked with him. It was time that he return home anyway, for a lawyer must, if he intends to practice, build a clientele in his earlier years. Many of these years had slipped by while he was in Washington. And Tom had been a good friend. When president of the student body at the university, he had appointed me to my first student government job.

Although he was not an integrationist by any means, he was not a rabble-rouser either. If change were to come to the South and Birmingham, he would be interested in its coming under law and with order. The city could escape an era of violence if King could lead it through the coming days of its upheaval.

Birmingham is not a "machine" town, but its politics are not as disorganized or unpredictable as Alabama politics statewide. Although no formal organization exists to dictate the direction of City Hall policy, a kind of Consensus does exercise a veto control over community affairs. The Consensus is composed of Birmingham industrial, banking, real estate and other important business leaders. Among themselves, without fuss or fanfare, these leaders reach agreement that this or that course of action or the election of this or that candidate is in the "best interests" of the city. Such agreements are not formalized, sometimes not even verbalized. At the country club, at a business lunch, over the telephone, the community leaders holding the purse strings and economic power simply make their opinions known to others. Or, without even saying so, everyone simply understands that in a given situation a particular course is desirable or undesirable.

Where community leaders are far-sighted, even an informal understanding reached on a golf course can start machinery in motion to solve a community problem. But Birmingham has suffered because its Consensus is essentially negative in approaching political matters, more interested in blocking threats to its interests than pushing positive programs or candidates. History had shown that so long as the policies and men at City Hall did not pose a threat to Consensus interests, the membership really did not give a damn whether Tweedledee or Tweedledum occupied office space in City Hall. This allowed for wide latitude, from an affable, soft-spoken mayor like Jimmie Morgan to a vociferous segregationist police commissioner like Bull Conner. Up to 1961, apathy, not virulent reaction, had been the primary barrier to progress in Birmingham.

In late 1960 King resigned his Washington job to return to Birmingham. He joined forces with my partner and me. Soon he was busy handling cases and sounding out community sentiment on his political future.

From the people who had shared Tom's university years a campaign organization sprang up, forward-looking, dedicated and aggressive. The King campaign brought together in common cause young men who had remained South to help build a better region and community. These were the "leaders of tomorrow" who did not choose to move North, West or East for opportunity, but who wanted to create opportunity at home.

Tomorrow had arrived—but the older heads who had enjoyed their oratorical flourish at our high school commencement exercises in former years were not at all pleased that their words were being taken seriously.

Past experience seemed to argue against it, but the Tom King campaign held out one more glowing hope that Birmingham might realize better days. Other cities had awakened from community lethargy when young men sounded the alarm. This might be Birmingham's time for change. Regardless of past experience, for Birminghamians who wanted to move their city ahead, there was nothing to lose. This became a crusade for good government, led by a new generation. Many of my friends disagreed with my developing views on how to deal with our city's problems—especially our urgent racial problem—but on one issue there was no argument: Tom King would provide vigorous leadership in attracting needed industry and business for our community's stagnating economy.

King's principal opponent was Arthur J. Hanes. Hanes had been employed as security officer at Hayes International, an aircraft manufacturer and one of the city's largest employers—second only to the Tennessee Coal and Iron Division of U.S. Steel. Like Tom, Art Hanes had family roots in Birmingham. Among his qualifications for office, he had served as president of the city's board of education. The board's activities fell within Bull Connor's City Hall jurisdiction. After Connor's own re-election was assured, Hanes would receive powerful backing from the police commissioner as well as from outgoing Mayor Morgan.

Tom's long absence from the community made him an underdog at the outset of the campaign, but the enthusiasm of his supporters, a skillful publicity and advertising campaign and his own dogged persistence soon attracted the interest of some of the city's more progressive businessmen.

Real estate developers, downtown merchants and others directly hurt by Birmingham's economic stagnation were searching for a fresh approach to community affairs. King was not satisfied with the status quo and he therefore became the candidate of those who sought change, including local leaders of organized labor and the city's Negro voters.

Conversely, as his campaign picked up steam, Tom's threat to the status quo upset many conservative business and political interests. Early in the campaign he was invited to speak before the air transportation committee of the Chamber of Commerce. He jolted the group with blunt criticism of the city's efforts to get better air service. A local joke concerning this problem runs, "If I die and go to hell, I'll have to lay over in Atlanta," and Tom told the C. of C. members that Birmingham had fallen behind other Southeastern communities in preparing for the jet age. He concluded that this failure was the result of short-sighted planning and that it cramped the area's economic growth.

Within hours a prominent Chamber of Commerce official attacked King's statement and issued a blanket defense of the city's air transport program. For his part, Art Hanes sided with those who defended the city's rate of progress in air transportation and in other economic areas. Before the campaign was over, Hanes attacked King for wanting "to make Birmingham into another Atlanta." The argument was that Atlanta's progress came at too high a cost: Integration.

Thus Tom King, born and reared in the Birmingham area —whose time outside Birmingham was spent in uniform overseas and serving community needs in the local Congressman's Washington office—was to find himself attacked as an

[91]

"outsider," sent down from Washington (some said by the Kennedy administration itself) to prepare Birmingham's "surrender" to federal integration programs.

A city too can suffer psychological problems and Birmingham's years of tension seemed to be taking a toll. The community seemed to me to be losing all touch with the reality of the world outside Jefferson County and Alabama—and even reality as it existed within its boundaries.

For a long period of time we had come to accept the fact that certain television presentations—those which dealt with racial problems in a way that local station operators felt might affect the community adversely—were simply not shown to area audiences. Similarly our newspapers often found it in the community interest to feature certain kinds of stories concerning the race problem and to submerge, or even eliminate, other kinds.

The community was being given only that aspect of the race problem that the communications media thought it should hear—or thought that it could hear without repercussions from the extreme elements. The cutting of television cables to prevent "offensive" national shows from being presented was one potential form of extremist protest. The fact that some shows not even concerned with the race problem, e.g., variety shows like Ed Sullivan's, often used Negro performers was a source of outrage for others. Their argument was that national television had a responsibility not to offend the sensibilities of its viewers, and when Ed Sullivan puts a Negro on his show he is, in effect, inviting that person into the viewers' homes. This opinion might be considered absurd by an overwhelming majority of Birmingham and Alabama television viewers, but the fact that a sizable percentage of the population felt that way ultimately affected the outlook of the communications media. In this way the most extreme elements were setting the standards for community acceptance or rejection of information and even entertainment.

Moreover, the almost total absorption of the city in the single problem of race over a long period, to the exclusion of other national and international problems, could not help but distort the total community's outlook and sense of values. And so a mythology, complete with demons, was emerging to explain away our city's trials and tribulations. The Hughes case had provided an insight into how the workings of this mythology affected individual rights, and now the King campaign was to demonstrate, to a degree greater than ever before, its political efficacy.

As with the other young men and women involved in the campaign, for me the long nights of the early spring developed into months of absorption. The organization functioned well, and although it sometimes made mistakes the campaign itself successfully captured the city's imagination.

Birmingham had dreams now and they were presented in the person of a young man attacking the status quo, proposing plans for an expanded and forward-looking city—one in which we could all live and work and thrive and prosper. All candidates declared that they would maintain segregation in city institutions and emphasized other issues. Birmingham's electoral mind for a few brief weeks left its thoughts of race behind. And there was hope again.

Tom surprised the experts by leading the seven-man field

in the first primary. Hanes, who had been favored, ran second. Now, in a two-man, head-to-head contest, the race issue became dominant.

The number of Negroes voting in Birmingham is small relative to the size of the Negro population. However, in a close election the city's eight to ten thousand Negro votes could prove decisive. In first primary campaigns, where three or more candidates vie for enough votes to get into a two-man run-off, few go out of their way to repudiate or alienate the Negro vote. When evidence grew that the 1961 first primary would be close, Art Hanes even told a downtown luncheon club audience that he would accept the votes of a number of groups, including the NAACP and the KKK—and any other support that came his way. He would not be particular; a vote was a vote.

But when Tom King carried the predominantly Negro boxes in the first primary, Hanes became particular. He repudiated the Negro vote he had not received and based his run-off campaign on the white voters' need to defeat "the NAACP bloc vote." The four-week run-off period would find Tom King subjected to what professional politicians in the area term "the black hand" treatment.

In Birmingham the precincts where many Negroes vote are gerrymandered to isolate their influence. The candidate who receives Negro support—which, like minority support anywhere in the country, tends to move solidly behind one candidate in a given election—is therefore easily identified by studying returns from specific boxes. The Legion Field box near downtown Birmingham is the best-known local indicator. Thus, cynical politicians advise that if a candidate is going to get Negro votes, he should make sure he gets them only in the run-off. If he gets them in the first primary and must then go into a run-off campaign, his opponent will make his Negro support a liability issue. Newspaper advertisements and circulars showing a black hand placing a ballot in a box, with a bold headline warning, "Defeat the NAACP Bloc Vote," is the standard technique employed. This was the nature of the campaign aimed against Tom King's candidacy in the June, 1961, mayoralty run-off.

But, although the race issue was known to cut deep, odds still favored King's election. He had several factors working for his success, the most important being a fifteen-hundred-vote lead over Hanes in the first primary. Most of the also-rans threw their support to King, as did the *News* (owned, according to Hanes, by outsider *"Samuel Isaac Newhouse"*). Hanes' principal support came from Bull Connor, and other entrenched interests. In addition the Scripps-Howard-owned *Post Herald,* which had backed a losing hard-line segregationist in the first primary, now gave its editorial support to Hanes.

It was to blunt the horns of Hanes' strongest political supporter that King went to City Hall to visit Bull Connor early in the run-off. Tom hoped to neutralize the commissioner, but the effort proved futile. Then, with the photograph of King shaking hands with a Negro, a volatile new factor entered into election calculations.

A study of the picture revealed landmarks and other evidence establishing that it had been taken from a City Hall window. In looking at the photo I was struck by the special irony of the message painted on the sidewalk where King and his unknown caller were standing. The sidewalk message read: "Stop fires—save lives." For Tom King and his campaign supporters, the fires of racist politics had now been lit —and there were forces at work to fan the flames.

I had become "controversial," and to be "controversial" in Birmingham connotes not so much a penchant for controversy as for being on the unpopular side of a controversy. In terms of the campaign, this meant that I made fewer public appearances on behalf of the candidate and concentrated more on organizational work. In the closing days of the run-off, smear sheets circulated associating me with the King campaign and pointing out that I was the lawyer who had represented Bob Hughes.

To Tom's credit, the character of opposition attacks only stiffened his will to win. He did not scare easily. But other advice around him was that in order to win he would have to "fight fire with fire," and as the campaign progressed the King campaign itself became immersed in the politics of "Seg." It was 1958 and 1959 all over again. My opinion was reconfirmed that even for well-intentioned candidates the state's politics had become a trap. This would be the last political campaign in which I really hoped to see any candidate—including my own—escape the trap.

During the King-Connor meeting the commissioner mentioned that a Freedom Rider bus was coming to Birmingham. Its arrival on Mother's Day was to prove a turning point in the campaign—and in the nation's civil rights movement. One bus was met at Anniston, Alabama, and burned. The other bus was met at the downtown Birmingham Trailways station by a polyglot assortment of white toughs, many of them from outside the city. The station is only a few blocks away from City Hall and police headquarters, but Bull Connor's men arrived too late at the scene to prevent a bloody incident. The riders were beaten, and local news and television reporters were also attacked.

On the following day the Birmingham *News* ran a front-page editorial asking: Where were the police? The *Post-Herald* joined in expressing its editorial outrage. The city was shocked, ashamed, indignant. But within days, after the world outside Birmingham also expressed shock and indignation, the community reverted to its old defensive pattern. Now the indignation was directed at other targets.

People in trouble must find someone to blame. President Kennedy had been in office for less than four months but it was on him that Birmingham, and much of the South, had already fixed its sights. He was the man to be blamed for every grievance, real or fancied.

The city had not voted for a Democratic nominee for President since 1944. It could not be expected to feel kinship with the man who last defeated its electoral judgment. But the President's younger brother was to be the principal target. Simply because he was young and Roman Catholic and Attorney General he was a marked man. And now it was easy for the politicians to say that he had started the Freedom Ride; he had caused the trouble. And, "after all, King had worked in Washington, hadn't he?"

A pyramid of hatred was being erected in the South. Its base was to be the Kennedy administration, its walls reaction to men seeking their constitutional rights. Riots at bus stations in Birmingham and Montgomery and afterward at Oxford and hundreds of demonstrations at lunch counters across the South would provide the energy for its construction.

The question of where the police had been remained unanswered. What became important was the extent to which Attorney General Robert F. Kennedy had assisted the Freedom Riders.

From Birmingham, the Freedom Riders were driven under escort to the state line of Tennessee. But they returned to Birmingham, then drove on to Montgomery, where new rioting broke out and a horde of U.S. marshals were sent in to contain the mobs. The National Guard was called out. Every newscast, every front-page headline, told of new incidents concerning race riots and violence.

The political atmosphere was highly charged and the final days of the mayoralty run-off campaign were desperate ones for both camps. But now the King campaign was in trouble. The race issue blotted out all talk of Tom King's program for economic growth. Connor and Hanes blamed the Mother's Day riot on outside agitators looking for trouble. Hanes pointed to the incident to support his argument that the NAACP had organizational designs on Birmingham.

And from the citizens around whom this controversy turned—Birmingham's Negroes—silence. The white community believes that the Negro equal rights movement is monolithic. To the white Birminghamian, it is inconceivable that Birmingham Negro leaders and the Freedom Riders were not following a single battle plan. Yet the evidence is otherwise. The Freedom Riders' timing proved disastrous for those members of the community, white and Negro alike, who were hoping for a more progressive day in Birmingham city government. Like the Reichstag fire of a former day, if there had been no Freedom Ride there were those in Birmingham who might have wished to invent one.

Tom King lost by slightly more than three thousand votes. It was a bitter loss to the young group that had worked to create a brighter future for their home town. It was a bitter loss to all moderate elements in the community. But events had combined once again to keep Birmingham bound by its past fears instead of impelled by its future hopes. Our city had become less a community than a battlefield where forces of change and reaction were to clash.

Two years later, Tom King again ran for mayor under a new city council form of government. He ran third. Albert Boutwell led the field and Bull Connor was runner-up. In the run-off, Boutwell, the favored candidate of the Consensus, finally defeated Connor—but only by a margin roughly approximating the city's Negro vote.

Tom King's political education was complete: As the cynics say, if you're going to get their votes, make sure you get them in the run-off.

The Black Belt, Ballots and Them Plugged-Up Holes

My POLITICAL EDUCATION had also been completed. And, reflecting on the experiences of the King campaign, I became more convinced than ever that change for Birmingham would not—probably could not—come in the arena of the electorate. The city was locked into a box—its every avenue of escape blocked by the vote of a majority of its white population. Yet, if Birmingham was trapped, so was I. This was my home and the home of my family, but it was engaged in a suicidal rendezvous with its own past. If this were to be the home I wanted for myself and my family, either the city or I would have to change. Actually we both were changing. Birmingham was driven—whether by shame or guilt or laziness didn't really matter—to a new hardness, a new tolerance of its worst elements. It seemed to be constantly relearning to close its eyes to the worst of its atrocities and to smile, understandingly, at the least of them. On the contrary, I could not do this, and I was being driven more and more apart from the city and the life I had hoped to lead. And, as each new case or campaign unfolded, as each victory or defeat occurred, the city and I found ourselves more and more often in the position of antagonists, not old friends.

I dissolved my law partnership—there was no need to burden others further with the onus of my growing disagreement with Birmingham. From now on I would try it alone. But in a legal struggle to wrest control of Alabama from the Black Belt I was to find allies.

The Black Belt, named for the richness of its soil rather than the color of most of its people, is the antebellum plantation and slaveholding region of Alabama.

In 1901 our white political leaders rewrote the state's constitution. Their aim was to forever remove Negroes from the voter rolls. At the convention Black Belt politicians shrewdly insisted that even though the Negroes were to be disenfranchised they should be counted when allocating the number of state representatives or senators a county was to receive. Consequently the Black Belt continued its traditional control of state government even though the overwhelming majority of its citizens could not vote. Politically archconservative and the heartland of the state's Dixiecrat sentiment, it dominated Alabama political affairs for over half a century, thanks to its leaders' refusal to reapportion the legislature in accordance with shifting population density.

Thus, sixty years after the framers of the state constitution had finished their work and returned to their sleepy rural, horse-drawn communities, most of Alabama's people lived from industrial Birmingham north to the Tennessee boundary —but political power still resided south, in the rural Black Belt. And most of that power lay outside of Mobile, South Alabama's largest, most progressive and most underrepresented city.

Northern capital that moves South—smart Northern capital—soon learns how to live in peace and harmony with Southern hosts, especially those hosts that hold the reins of political power. Long years ago an alliance had been struck between conservative Birmingham business, whose outlook was that of Northern Big Steel, and conservative Black Belt power. Urban-rural differences were submerged in order that these established interests could form a common political front against the restive, growing and "radical" Populist counties of North Alabama.

Tax exemptions for industrial machinery and a hostile legislative climate for organized labor benefited Birmingham business; low property tax rates on land and a disproportionate share of the state's tax dollars benefited the Black Belt. And there were other mutual benefits of the alliance. Birmingham's leaders paid lip service to the reapportionment issue, but crucial power tests nearly always found the Big City and the Black Belt joining forces.

Nevertheless, the people of Birmingham and North Alabama had only to consider population statistics to realize how the existing situation limited their voice in state government. In the Birmingham area, one state senator represented 634,000 people; in the Black Belt county of Lowndes, one state senator represented only 15,000 people. In varying degrees, the same inequality existed between many populous North Alabama counties and the Black Belt.

Other factors worked to retard the state's progress, but there was no doubt in my mind that Black Belt domination in Montgomery was the vital political underpinning to a system designed to curb the influence of all the state's Negroes and a major part of its more progressive white population. For north of Birmingham reside the citizens of the Tennessee Valley region and Huntsville—Alabamians whose lives are directed toward a future influenced by TVA and the Redstone Arsenal rather than the glories of a past century. If these North Alabamians could be given their proper voice in state affairs, it seemed to me the climate of our politics would change and Alabama might fulfill the rich promise of its forward-looking people and its natural resources.

The summer of 1961 found the state in a political furor. The 1960 census figures required that Alabama lose one of its Congressmen.

With only a trace of a smile the old-hand political pros of the Black Belt devised an ingenious "chop-up" plan whereby the Birmingham area, like occupied Berlin, would be divided four ways among other Congressional districts. They argued that the big city folks wouldn't be losing one Congressman— we'd be getting four. But Birmingham's conservative business interests knew that three of the four were residents of liberal North Alabama. And they knew that their interests, always subject to Black Belt control in Montgomery, now would be unrepresented, to all intents and purposes, in Washington.

The "chop-up" came as a rude jolt to Birmingham's political and economic powers. They felt betrayed. Their tryst with the Black Belt was over, at least temporarily, and the Big Mules found themselves at war with their traditional allies. All of the power and prestige of Birmingham's business community was brought to bear on Montgomery. In the galleries and on the floor the lobbyists assembled and the battle of words began.

From the city's anger over the chop-up there emerged talk of a local suit to force reapportionment of the state legislature. Such a suit had been filed in Tennessee and was awaiting action by the Supreme Court of the United States. There was a story that the local Bar Association might initiate the action, but professional associations, legal, medical or otherwise, are slow to chart new political courses. Had the matter been left to a group of lawyers, the pioneers' decision to move west would still be on the agenda of the Philadelphia Bar Association.

Into the picture then stepped the Young Men's Business Club of Birmingham, the maverick of the city's business organizations. At a YMBC meeting, approval was given to initiate a group action in federal court to reapportion the Alabama legislature. I, along with George Peach Taylor and others, was chosen to represent the group.

We conferred with the attorneys in the Tennessee case, studied the law on the subject, prepared our suit—and waited.

We had expected that our suit would not be popularly received by Birmingham's power leadership even though they were angry over the chop-up. Their threat of a suit was no more than a threat and they knew that when the chop-up battle died down their divorce from the Black Belt could be set aside. Also, although it seemed ludicrous, fear of extremist reaction had come to pervade the community so thoroughly that even asking a federal court for the protection of our own constitutional rights was considered "unwise" by some people. Again I was urged, by conservatives and liberals alike, to exercise care and caution—in effect, to do nothing.

I had long since learned what advice of this sort led to in Birmingham. And I had too often seen its tragic results—the consequences of doing nothing about situations that were inequitable, undemocratic and unconstitutional. To some people, *now* is never the time and *this* is never the way. I ignored their advice, and when the chop-up debate reached a crucial point filed suit in the U.S. District Court in Montgomery, a beleaguered institution presided over by Frank M. Johnson, Jr.

Judge Johnson, tall, lean, in his early forties, was appointed to the bench by President Eisenhower. The two Democratic U.S. Senators from Alabama, Lister Hill and John J. Sparkman, did not oppose his nomination to the federal judgeship, but events were to prove that neither they nor the President was doing the young North Alabama Republican any real favor. To Judge Johnson's court would come the Montgomery bus boycott case, the Freedom Rider cases and other heated racial controversies.

A former law school classmate of gubernatorial candidate Judge George Wallace, Johnson had incurred Wallace's hostility. Wallace had stated that if FBI men, federal "snoopers," came into his judicial circuit he was going to jail them. Despite Wallace's threat they came seeking the voter registration records of Bullock County. Wallace publicly announced that the "Feds" would not get the voter records and he turned them over to the local grand jury. Judge Johnson ordered

Wallace to release the records to the investigators but Wallace publicly proclaimed that he would not abide by Judge Johnson's order. Wallace jousted with the order, getting headlines across the state, and Johnson had no choice but to cite him for contempt of court. But by the time Wallace came to trial the voter records had been placed in the hands of federal investigators. On the grounds that Wallace, regardless of his public utterances, had surreptitiously surrendered the records to agents of the United States, Judge Johnson found Wallace "not guilty." Rarely, if ever, has a defendant found "not guilty" confessed his guilt so loudly, for a "not guilty" Wallace was a candidate in serious political trouble. Wallace publicly protested that he had not turned the voter records over to the United States. He publicly insisted he had defied the federal order. During the 1962 gubernatorial campaign, Wallace protested that anyone who said he had complied, meaning Judge Johnson, was an "integrating, scalawagging. carpetbagging, bald-faced liar." Clearly, Frank Johnson upset some people in Montgomery and South Alabama.

Nevertheless, assigned to represent the federal judicial power in a community and area increasingly resentful of this power, Judge Johnson met his duty. His Northwest Alabama background may provide part of the reason. At the time of the outbreak of the Civil War, the Northwest county of Winston split on the question of slavery, seceded from the State of Alabama and declared itself a pro-Union "Free State of Winston." The secession was crushed by state Confederate authorities, but the heritage has been passed down—to the lone Republican representative in the legislature that Winston County many times has sent to Montgomery to do battle with 105 Democrats; and to independent, proud men like

Frank Johnson, one century later a pro-Union loner in a society hostile to federal law and authority.

Meanwhile, the political and economic powers of "Imperial Jefferson" had rallied to save the Birmingham Congressional District from dismemberment at the hands of its erstwhile Black Belt allies. Indeed, the years of alliance had taught the Big City boys some of the tricks of the legislative trade. The Black Belters pushing the chop-up plan were to find themselves hoist by their own petard: the filibuster. Black Belt filibusters, like filibusters in Washington, had stalled and defeated legislation in former years. Now Birmingham's lone state senator, Lawrence Dumas, Jr., a senior member of the law firm for which I had first worked, was joined by a handful of his non-Black Belt colleagues in a desperate effort to run out the legislative clock and kill the bill. They succeeded in defeating the chop-up and substituting in its place a redistricting plan whereby our nine incumbent Congressmen would run for eight positions on a statewide basis—the man receiving the least number of votes being eliminated from the delegation.

But the Black Belt had opened a Pandora's box, and the defeat of the chop-up plan did not mean the end of our push for reapportionment. Nor did it mean the end of support for our position by the more progressive elements of the business community. The powerful Birmingham *News* had entered our corner when the suit was filed. It stayed there until the battle was over. On March 26, 1962, the Supreme Court of the United States delivered its ruling in *Baker vs. Carr,* the Tennessee case; federal courts had jurisdiction in state reapportionment cases. Three days later, we filed a motion to enjoin the entire May Democratic primary election so that the legislature, like our Congressmen, would be elected state-at-large. In this manner we hoped to force the state legislators into reapportionment themselves. Few politicians relish the expenditure of time and money required by a state-at-large election. And, if the election were held on a statewide basis it would be the populous areas which would elect a majority of legislators. But, most importantly, the motion was filed simply to bring the case to a head and enable the court to get on with whatever action it felt was warranted.

A three-judge panel had been called together in Judge Johnson's court in Montgomery to hear our reapportionment case. Other members of the panel, besides Judge Johnson, were Judge Richard T. Rives of the U.S. Circuit Court of Appeals in New Orleans, and District Judge Daniel H. Thomas of Mobile. Since Judge Rives lived in Montgomery, all members of the panel were familiar with the Alabama political and legislative situation.

Two weeks after filing the motion we were in court. There I argued that the state had been totally dominated for sixty years by an illegally constituted legislature and that *now* was the time to end minority Black Belt domination of our state. I contended that the voice of "one boll weevil" in the Black Belt was heard more clearly in Montgomery than the combined voices of the more progressive-minded people of Alabama. The arguments ended and the panel adjourned for thirty minutes. I stood outside in the crowded hall and chatted with Camille and Charles and my mother and father, who had driven down from Birmingham to hear me argue this case. A murmur in the hallway signalled our return to the courtroom. The crowd stood and the three judges took their seats behind the bench. Unless the legislature acted voluntarily the judges felt they would "be under a clear duty to take some action in time to take effect before the general election of November 1962," Judge Rives read from the bench. The state legislature had until July 16, 1962, to do the job—otherwise, the court would do it.

As we left the courtroom a young reporter with the Birmingham *Post-Herald* turned to me. "It makes you feel good to know you still live in the United States," he said softly. "Yes, sir, it makes you feel damned good to know you live in the United States of America."

The structure of Black Belt political dominance was tottering. Governor Patterson called a special session of the legislature and the legislators hurried to Montgomery. Now they were not concerned with the chop-up of a Congressional seat but with a statewide chop-up of their own political domain. Five decades of obstruction and foot dragging were nearing an end.

The United States District Court in Birmingham had ordered that the city's sixty-eight parks, thirty-eight playgrounds, six swimming pools and four golf courses be desegrated. But the recently elected city fathers stood by their pledge to maintain segregation at all costs. They simply closed the parks. Birmingham's mayor, Art Hanes, called an open meeting to discuss the commission's decision.

Several of us from the YMBC were asked by some of the city's older well-established businessmen to join them at City Hall and attend the evening meeting. The older businessmen, as though in keeping with a tradition requiring absence at places of controversy, never arrived.

Inside the modern marble commission chamber a large crowd studded with burly men garbed in sweat shirts sat silently waiting for the meeting to begin.

A little gray-haired lady in the audience rose and questioned the mayor about the effect of closed parks on the problem of juvenile delinquency. She had come as a representative from her church circle. "Sit down and shut up," someone in the crowd shouted.

"Nigger lover" greeted the young salesman who rose to suggest that the parks remain open for Little League use. The taunt came from someone sitting near the wall which bore the inscription "Cities Are What Men Make Them."

David Baker, a young lawyer now practicing in New York, rose to speak.

"Does the city really think it can stand up against the courts and the strength of the United States government?" he asked. "And, if so, what chance does the United States have against Russia?"

I was sitting behind Baker on the middle aisle near the center of the room. A bulky man in a sweat shirt stormed by me. He turned on the nonplused Baker, his face contorted with hatred, and shook his fist.

"You ain't nothin' but a Jew," he sputtered. "You ain't nothin' but a goddamned Greek Jew." He paused as though out of breath. And then, almost as an afterthought, he shouted, "You don't even talk right."

The hall, previously very noisy, was now silent. As though nothing had happened the man turned and went back to his seat in the rear. And Harvard-educated David Baker sat down.

I knew that the protests were almost over now. If no one

spoke the other side would have won complete control of the meeting. I stood up. I allowed that I didn't intend to be interrupted or intimidated. The mayor called for order. I told the mayor that, as he knew, I had been a leader in the move to merge Mountain Brook into Birmingham. "What effect, if any, do you think closing the parks will have on the merger movement?" I asked. After a long response, the essence of which was "none," I sat down.

"I'm going to expose that man," came the cry from the back of the room. "Ask him if he didn't defend that nigger-loving preacher out in Bessemer."

I rose, the mayor cautioned we ought not enter into personalities, and I answered the man quietly and affirmatively. I suggested to him that the time might come when he would also need a lawyer. He shouted that the lawyer wouldn't be me. I responded that that was good news.

A short while later the meeting broke up. As we left City Hall I knew that I'd done it again. The tough-looking faces in the crowd now appeared in the hall clustered in knots talking in subdued tones. We walked past them into the elevators and down into the night. "Tough-looking bunch," someone said. And he was right.

After the meetings at City Hall I was subjected to a new spate of telephone calls. And this seemed a rougher breed of callers—if anonymous voices can be placed into categories.

Finally, one night, as much in desperation as anger, I called one of the city's leading segregationists. When I was certain he was as awake as I was I told him that I'd just received another threatening call. And to his protests at being wakened I told him that I knew he would be interested in learning of each and every threat I received. Consequently

I was going to telephone him whenever I received an anonymous call, day or night. The calls came less frequently then. But the temper of the city seemed to be growing shorter. I had floodlights installed around the house.

In the hot and muggy Montgomery of July, 1962, sixty-one years after the Constitutional Convention of 1901, the Alabama legislature was finally reapportioned. The legislature adopted two plans. We contended that neither of them was satisfactory. The court modified the legislature's plans and ordered an immediate reapportionment. Overnight the size of the Jefferson County house delegation grew from seven to seventeen members. It had not been an easy task for either the court or the legislature—and it had certainly not been a smooth road for those of us who handled the litigation. Ahead lay an appeal—ultimately the Supreme Court was to hear the case. But the time had proven right. And the way had been proven right. Despite the doubters, the voice of the people was to be more clearly heard in Montgomery.

But in Birmingham the parks remained closed. A short-lived and futile dissent was registered by Birmingham's golfing community. Without greenkeepers, pros and caddies they continued to frequent the municipal courses. But one day workmen appeared on the scene and very carefully filled the holes on each green.

Thus, a breach in the dike of segregation was blocked. That's the way it always had happened in Birmingham. All that the segregationists had to do was "go out and plug up them holes."

X

The Roots of Wrath

"I THOUGHT HE WAS DRUNK," the witness driving from work said. "I stopped my car and watched him stagger around for some time," he continued. "I drove off and about seven blocks down the street I decided to telephone police."

The place: a Bush Oil Company Service Station, Seventh Street and First Avenue North, Birmingham. The time: Sunday evening, June 3, 1962. The event: the death by clubbing with a blunt instrument of Fred Andrews Reed, age twenty-five, white service station attendant.

Moments later a pick-up truck ran a red light at Sixteenth Street and Eighth Avenue North. Police stopped it. The driver, a Negro man, escaped and dashed into the night. A billfold was dropped. Police found it.

Two days later Boaz Melvin Sanders, "age 25, black, male," as the Birmingham police blotter described him, was arrested and charged with murder and robbery. The Birmingham *News* alleged that he confessed to the crimes.

From June through October of 1962 I served as Sanders' court-appointed defense attorney in a case in which he stood accused of two separate offenses each punishable by death in the electric chair.

From its outset, the Sanders matter presented, in the words of the trial judge, "a peculiar case." It opened on a note of challenge—to the Birmingham area's circuit solicitor, to the judge, to the Alabama criminal law system as a whole.

In May, 1962, the U.S. Fifth Circuit Court of Appeals, in the case of *Seals vs. Wiman,* set aside the death-penalty rape conviction of Negro defendant Willie Seals because Negroes had been systematically excluded from his trial jury. This ruling was not novel, in itself. What was different was that the reversal was ordered despite the fact that the point had not been raised during the trial by a white court-appointed attorney. Following conviction, and appeals through the state court system, Seals obtained Negro lawyers. They had filed a habeas corpus petition in federal court raising the juror question.

In yet another death-penalty case, the Supreme Court of the United States had reversed the conviction of Charles Clarence Hamilton, a Negro, sending it back to Jefferson County, Alabama, for retrial. The defendant, said the Supreme Court, had not been provided with legal counsel at every stage of his criminal proceeding.

State Circuit Judge Wallace Gibson of Birmingham was familiar with the rulings in the Seals and Hamilton cases. As a conscientious jurist, Judge Gibson does not like being

reversed by higher courts. As an Alabama judge, he no doubt
has a special dislike for being reversed by federal courts. To
Judge Gibson, the case of *State of Alabama vs. Boaz Melvin
Sanders,* coming on the heels of the Seals and Hamilton
rulings, must have raised juridical storm warnings.

The judge, along with the office of Circuit Solicitor
Emmett Perry, wanted the Sanders case tried on its merits
in a manner that would stand up under appeal if conviction were obtained. Neither the judge nor the prosecutor
wanted unfairness in the trial of a criminal case. The defendant, an indigent who said he could not afford counsel, would
have to be represented by someone willing to raise every
constitutional defense in his behalf. In early June, with the
circuit court about to recess for the summer, Judge Gibson
was responsible for assuring that Sanders had legal representation and, as the judge was quoted in the *News,* that he also
had "every opportunity to challenge any and all actions in
his case, including motions questioning the make-up of the
grand jury."

On June 11, Judge Gibson requested that I take the case.
Under Alabama law, the fee would be $100, the amount paid
court-appointed attorneys in a capital case.

Between the demands of my regular practice and the reapportionment case, I was already pressed for time. Yet the
Sanders case posed a challenge that could not be refused,
though it might again lead to threats from anonymous
strangers, headshaking from good friends and querulous looks
from regular clients. I accepted the case and immediately
moved to delay the trial until the fall so that a complete
defense could be prepared. Judge Gibson granted the motion.

Then began a study of Alabama's criminal jurisprudence and the effect of racial segregation on the constitutional rights of Negro defendants. I set out to study every detail, to question every aspect of the system. No rule or custom of court would be taken for granted as constitutionally correct simply because it was "the way things are done around here."

My first conclusion was that challenging the composition of juries in the county was in itself not sufficient to guarantee my client's rights. Suppose a single Negro could become a member of the Boaz Sanders trial jury? How effective could he be in a panel with eleven Alabama white men? I noted with special interest a Montgomery newspaper report concerning a meeting of state circuit solicitors and their discussion of the Negro juror question. "One prosecuting attorney," according to the report, "said he recalled a case in which eleven white men on the jury decided the suit on the basis of which side, in their opinion, put the twelfth juror, a Negro, in the jury box."

No, the systematic exclusion of Negroes from juries was only one element that might deny due process and equal protection to a Negro defendant in Alabama. The operation of our jury system was but a single thread woven through the whole fabric of segregation as a way of life and a social order. Directly and indirectly, consciously and unconsciously, by ways both harsh and subtle, our state's legal system reflected and provided the bulwark for a social system that treated Negroes as lower-caste citizens.

Talks with psychiatrists and psychologists served to confirm my conclusion: the social attitudes of the community had created two separate concepts of justice, one applying to

whites, another to Negroes—in much the same way that we
provided two separate kinds of drinking fountains in our
courthouse and racially segregated audiences in our court-
rooms. It was as simple as the fact that while jurors considering a case heard white witnesses called "Mr." or "Mrs.,"
Negro witnesses were called "Sam" or "Mary," on a patron-
izing first-name basis. Finally, after exhaustive research and
preparation, I was ready to submit my motion to quash the
indictment against Boaz Sanders.

In mid-August Camille and I traveled south to Mobile for
a brief reunion cruise on the Gulf of Mexico with old college friends. It was an occasion for regaining perspective on
where we had been and where we might be headed. For an
inland Alabamian—an indoor-type inlander, at that—a visit
to the Gulf can be a tonic. For that matter, Mobile itself, an
Alabama community with tradition and style, offered a re-
laxing contrast with our own home town. Here was the oldest
inhabited section of Alabama, a Deep Southern community
with a proportionately larger Negro population. Yet it was
not suffering Birmingham's self-destructive ordeal. On the
trip back, driving through the low coastal flatlands toward
the rolling red hills of Central Alabama, I puzzled over the
enigma: Which city was the real South, and which citizens
could lay true claim to that cherished illusion, the Southern
heritage? Were Mobile and Atlanta somehow less "Southern"
than strife-torn Albany and Birmingham?

We enjoyed our cruise. But most of these old friends from
college days had moved from Birmingham and we saw those
remaining only on rare occasions. The young couples from

apartment days had gone their own ways and our paths rarely crossed.

But there was one feature of life in Birmingham that made living there often pleasant. The dissenters from the community's mores had gathered together. Over the years those who wanted change in the community met each other at parties or bridge or at church or work. And, when the conversation of strangers politely drifted to race, as it almost always did, the dissenters identified each other. There grew among them a closeness that led to parties and conversation during the difficult years. Doctors and lawyers, teachers and preachers, young bankers, businessmen and journalists, and their wives came to recognize the one intangible bond which held them together—they disagreed with Birmingham. And even if their disagreement with the city was a quiet and private matter, when their invitations went out we were included. Probably never again were all of us to belong to a group of friends so closely knit.

The Sanders motion was filed. At the outset, it argued that the State of Alabama does not provide an indigent defendant with counsel early enough in the proceeding against him and even after appointment doesn't provide the attorney with sufficient funds to expend in the defense of the client.

"Such a system of justice insuring an adequate defense for the rich and a lame defense for the poor is no system of justice at all," this part of the motion concluded. "Boaz Sanders avers that this State cannot afford such squalid discrimination."

It was in the second section that I raised the basic issue

of the effect of Alabama's segregation laws and customs on the defendant's—or any Negro defendant's—constitutional right to a fair trial.

"Boaz Sanders, a Negro man, is accused of the crimes of both murder and robbery of a white man, the alleged acts having occurred on, to wit, the 3rd day of June, 1962," the motion recited. "He was arrested on the 5th day of June, 1962, by a white policeman or policemen, employed by the Police Department of the City of Birmingham, Alabama, the entire membership of which is composed of white men and women, Negroes being systematically excluded from employment therein because of race or color. . . ."

Thus began a step-by-step outline describing how racial segregation touched the lives and the rights of Negro prisoners in Birmingham, Alabama. Sanders was taken to jail "in a racially segregated patrol car or paddy wagon" as provided by a specific police department rule requiring that white and Negro prisoners cannot be transported "in the same compartment of the patrol wagon."

"He was then incarcerated in the City Jail of the City of Birmingham, all of the wardens, matrons, clerks, and employees of which are white, Negroes being systematically excluded from employment therein because of their race or color." And the prisoner was of course placed in segregated cell space. Transferred to the county jail, where the same conditions prevailed, he then was indicted by a grand jury, "Negroes having been systematically excluded from membership thereon."

Boaz Sanders was then arraigned, "brought to the courtroom by a white bailiff or other white court employee . . .

there being no Negro court employees in the Jefferson County (Birmingham Division) Courthouse.

"Approaching the said courtroom, he must pass by restrooms marked 'Colored Men' or 'Colored Women' or 'White Men' or 'White Women,'" the motion continued. "He also must pass drinking fountains, labeled 'Colored' and 'White.' . . ."

"On the sixth floor," the motion asserted, "he must pass by an elevator leading to the Law Library of the Birmingham Bar Association, which said Bar Association systematically excludes Negroes from membership therein. . . ."

Once in court, the Negro defendant would be tried by a white judge and prosecuted by a white solicitor—there being neither Negro judges nor Negro prosecutors in Alabama. His own lawyer would be white, as would his petit jury. But if one or more Negroes did appear on the petit jury in Sanders' case, "they would be required to use segregated restrooms, water fountains, eating facilities and overnight accommodations."

"Indeed, it would be impossible for a racially mixed petit jury to be kept together overnight in that there are no hotels, motels, restaurants, or other sleeping and eating places in Jefferson County, Alabama, whether publicly or privately owned, whereat a Negro member of a jury could be housed overnight and fed with other jury members who were white. . . ."

If convicted, segregated justice would follow the Negro defendant to the penitentiary—or to death row, where, if not freed on appeal through the all-white appellate courts, "he will be given a last meal by his white guards, shaved by a white barber, and taken by white guards to a yellow electric chair in Kilby Prison (the yellow electric chair being the only facility in Alabama justice which is and always has been desegregated, there being but one such electric chair in existence in the Alabama State penal institutions). A button or switch will then be pressed or pulled by a white man, before white witnesses, and the condemned man will die."

And finally—

"Being in indigent circumstances, he will thereafter be taken by white men and buried in a potter's grave in a racially segregated cemetery, provided by the State of Alabama. . . ."

After the legal attack was publicized in the local press, reaction was quick in coming. By this time, however, my secretary, Jane Gunthorpe, had developed an ingenuous technique for dealing with threatening callers.

"Tell your boss we're going to get him dead," were the exact words of the first caller on the morning following the Sanders motion.

"Thank you very much," replied Miss Gunthorpe, responding in best secretarial-school manner. "I'll give him the message."

On October 29, 1962, I was called to attend a hearing in the Sanders case. There I was surprised to learn that Sanders' mother had privately retained an attorney to represent him. Thus there was no further need for court-appointed counsel. As Judge Gibson said, "In other words, you would be, as of now, completely relieved of duty, and I will say this to you, Chuck, I want to thank you sincerely for the way in which you responded when I asked you to take on this job. It is a thankless job, as we mentioned at that time."

Five months after the Boaz Sanders case began it ended

like thousands of similar cases on the sixth floor of the Jefferson County courthouse. The accused entered a plea of guilty and what had been a constitutional question thereby became a criminological statistic.

Perhaps, as Judge Gibson told me at the time I turned over the Sanders file, it all added up to a "thankless job." But then again, Boaz Sanders' life had been spared. And, although my pleadings had been withdrawn in the state court by Sanders' family-retained attorney, a fundamental issue had been raised for the first time in open court in Alabama:

"The State of Alabama does not now and has not for many years (at least during this century) provided a system of justice other than the one set out herein which is based on absolute racial segregation," my motion concluded; "a segregation which permeates the entire system from the cradle to the grave; one from which Negroes are and have been systematically excluded in every respect except as defendants."

It is an issue that will be raised again someday—and dealt with. For the ideal of "Equal Justice for All Men" cannot be brushed aside if our society and the American system are to survive.

CHAPTER

XI

Blessed the Peacemaker

On APRIL 6, 1962, Big Jim Folsom arrived at the courthouse square in Talladega, to talk to the folks there about what he intended to do when elected to a third term as Alabama governor. Folsom was going into the stretch drive in what had become a desperate campaign to reverse the segregationist trend in state politics.

Known as a liberal by the state's political standards, Big Jim was running into pockets of audience coolness even in the branch-head areas where, during the campaigns of 1946 and 1954, he had been accepted as a country boy hero. The word was out that Folsom, now in his fifties and no longer the brash, bumptious "Kissin' Jim" who bussed the ladies during his first term, was "soft on segregation." In fact, Big Jim himself was stumping the state preaching harmony and, with the vocal help of his wife Jamelle, singing "Peace in the Valley."

The tone of the campaign was set early when Folsom's nephew, speaking for his uncle at a Black Belt political rally, answered a direct question on the Issue by declaring that "no man in his right mind can stand up here and say there will never be any integration." A reasonable enough statement—but vigorously challenged, right there on the spot, by an opposition spokesman.

Big Jim's opposition included: his former protégé George Wallace; Birmingham Police Commissioner Bull Connor; Attorney General MacDonald Gallion, along with Wallace and Connor regarded as a "hard-line segregationist"; Albert Boutwell, who was to drop out at a late stage of the race, but whose segregationist credentials included authorship of the Alabama Pupil Placement Law; and Ryan De Graffenried, a young Tuscaloosa state senator who offered a new face to voters.

Folsom's chances for a third term had been regarded as excellent at the outset of the campaign. It was thought that if anyone could overcome the racists' "black hand" attack he would be the man. But now, going into the final weeks, there were disturbing reports coming into the Folsom campaign entourage. Wallace was making headway with his pledge to "stand in the door" and personally bar Negro students from entry into previously all-white schools. Big Jim was being criticized for not sounding firm enough on the Issue. The Montgomery *Advertiser*—a capital newspaper that in both 1958 and 1962 found nothing inconsistent about supporting both a common-sense approach to racial problems *and* George Wallace for governor—was advising voters to back Wallace as the only candidate who could defeat Big Jim in a run-off. The appeal seemed to be catching on in many areas, including Talladega.

When Folsom got ready to speak at the courthouse square that April day, he was greeted not only by white citizens who had been waiting to hear him, but by Negro students from Talladega College. The students had come to the square to demonstrate for desegregation of public accommodations. The sight of Negro demonstrators publicly demanding an end to segregation laws in a small Alabama community must certainly have warned Big Jim and his supporters, if they did not already realize it, that much had changed since the successful campaigns of '46 and '54. And the changes were not only among white Alabamians. Of equal, perhaps greater, importance in the long run, young Alabama Negroes were shedding their parents' mask of docility, and growing increasingly militant.

The student demonstrations, timed as they were, further damaged Folsom's campaign chances. Oddly, had the same demonstrations been held when George Wallace came to town, his cause would have been helped. Under those circumstances, the students would have been viewed as protesting. But with Big Jim the opinion prevailed among the state's white voters that the Negroes were appealing to a friend for help. In former years, Negroes might have been dissuaded from doing anything that might embarrass a "white liberal friend." But the younger Negroes were having none of that "go slow" talk. Big Jim had always used the slogan "Y'all Come"—and when he arrived that day in Talladega they were there.

Folsom made his speech and moved on to the next town.

But the demonstrations continued, and, with the passage of days, grew in intensity. First, there had been a parade. Then came sit-ins, with the students entering local drugstores, seating themselves at counters and ordering soft drinks. As rapidly as they came, they were ordered to leave, and, upon refusing, they were escorted out to waiting patrol cars and jail. It was a pattern emerging throughout the South and the country.

Talladega College is a private Negro school. The leader of the demonstrators was a young singer, Dorothy Vails, who was president of the student body. She and others had planned student strategy. The demonstrators were carefully taught the technique of the sit-in, including how to protect themselves by covering their heads and vulnerable parts of their bodies if attacked. Actual lunch counter facsimiles were devised, chairs placed like counter stools. Some students acted the roles of waitresses, others of demonstrators. Every step of the nonviolent procedure was explained in detail.

For years, Talladega had prided itself on its "good race relations." Many Negroes were registered to vote and in past years there had even been Negro policemen—a practice since discontinued. The city itself was nestled comfortably around the courthouse square, looking much as it did in the days of the Old South. Community dissensions were few. The Negro college had operated for years and its students were good customers. There were no complaints about selling them sandwiches and soft drinks when they came into town—so long as they followed the time-honored custom of carrying the items outside the store. And they always had.

Clearly, to the white residents of Talladega, the demonstrators were either outside agitators or their movement was being spearheaded by outsiders. They simply were not "our kind" of Negro. "Our kind" of Negro was satisfied with his status in the community and the area. He paid his money inside, and ate his sandwiches outside.

As the demonstrations continued, the temper of the white community passed from incredulity to anger. There were more sit-ins, along with attempts to enter white movie houses. There were marches from campus to town. Pickets filled the sidewalks. Then, on Sunday, April 21, groups of Negro students attempted to enter six white churches around the city. At the Episcopal Church they were admitted and seated. At four churches they were turned away. And at Wesleyan Methodist Church, on that Easter Sunday morning, they were arrested and taken to jail.

As the two polarized elements in Talladega drew further apart, only one group in the area showed any desire to step into the dangerous middle ground. This was the Alabama Council on Human Relations, represented by the man who had succeeded Bob Hughes as executive director. He was a young, intense Baptist minister named Norman C. Jimerson.

A graduate of the University of Michigan, Jimerson was a Pacific theater Army veteran of World War II who had previously served as pastor in churches in Massachusetts and New Hampshire. In 1957 Jimerson became chaplain of the Federal Reformatory at Petersburg, Virginia, a position he held until he came to Birmingham in May of 1961.

Married, with five children, Jimerson's troubles with the Birmingham community began early—when he started looking for a home. Learning of Jimerson's work with the council, the real estate agent simply refused to sell to him. The agent told Jimerson that the Alabama council was a Communist organization and that his predecessor, Hughes, "was one of them." He urged Jimerson not to take the job, adding that if the minister accepted it, he must be a Communist too.

My role in the Hughes and subsequent cases seemed to have set my course as guardian in the community trials and tribulations of men like Jimerson. He telephoned me, and told me of his difficulties. I helped him find a place to live and drew up papers to close the transaction. But that was only the beginning of Norman Jimerson's problems.

As a Baptist minister, he desired to work with a Baptist church, although his primary assignment was with the council. He joined one, preached guest sermons—in which he did not mention race—and seemed to please the congregation. But, as information reached some of the membership about Jimerson's work with the Alabama council, pressure began building against his association with the church. Though the board of deacons voted against asking him to depart, private requests were made that he leave the church and save everyone embarrassment and trouble.

Shaken by this experience, Jimerson and his family began to attend a Presbyterian church and for a while made progress in becoming part of the community. He no longer was interested in a place to preach. He wanted a place to pray. But again his association with the council made him a target for segregationist attack. Soon a movement was under way to exclude him from membership with his new church. He was advised to talk with one of the prominent men of the parish, a top-level corporate executive. At the meeting, he was asked if he was a Communist. "No," he responded, "I am a Christian." From that point, the interview continued downhill for two hours, with the executive inquiring as to the nature of Jimerson's faith, his past and his work with the council. But finally the minister's inquisitor was satisfied: he would not go along with any vote to exclude Jimerson from the church.

"I won't vote," he said. "I'll abstain."

So it was in Birmingham; among the decent leaders of the community, neither the ayes nor the nays, but the abstentions had it. When Jimerson related this story, I told him that the executive's position unfortunately reflected the community's essential moral problem—not the action of "extremists" who attack, but the inaction of "moderates" who abstain. Jimerson next learned that his social contacts were under pressure from hostile community elements—"on the spot," as one friend told him. Rumors spread that he was under investigation by various private sources. Now, as a layman, he was being asked to leave his new church for the same reasons he had left the Baptist congregation. I appeared on his behalf before the board of elders of a second Presbyterian parish with which he had affiliated, but to no avail. We were told that his mere presence would make problems for an already splintered congregation.

Like a modern-day Job, Jimerson seemed to take from his ordeals an increased strength and faith in the Christian peacemaking aims of the Alabama council. As executive director, his work did not include either participation in or encouragement of racial demonstrations. He was to serve as the mediator, the negotiator, the peacemaker. The council believed that racial progress was better made at the bargaining table than in the streets.

When the Talladega demonstrations began, Jimerson had gone to the city, forty-five miles from Birmingham, to attempt to establish communications between Negroes and the community's white leadership. He made an effort to talk to the mayor, to members of the police department, to local businessmen, to several local ministers and to Dr. Arthur Gray, president of Talladega College. Jimerson learned quickly that Negro college students in Alabama, as across the nation, had shoved their way past their elders in order to move into the streets. Dr. Gray's influence, even had he exerted it to the fullest, would not have been enough to halt the demonstrations. The peacemaker would have to stand between Negro militants and white intransigents. Under similar circumstances, Big Jim Folsom simply struck up "Peace in the Valley" for two choruses and moved on to the next town. The preacher would be forced to face his ordeal within rather than outside the courthouse.

Jimerson's meeting with the local ministerial association proved frustrating. The membership concerned itself solely with a resolution condemning racial unrest in the community —and with the presence of Jimerson, "an outsider," at the meeting. But the man who would be peacemaker learns patience. Jimerson persisted, going to the homes of several white ministers to talk to them privately, asking their help in opening up racial communications lines to settle racial unrest. His patience was to go unrewarded. The demonstrations continued and he went home. Days later Jimerson again arrived in Talledega to attempt a reconciliation of the opposing forces. Community feeling among both whites and Negroes had grown more tense and positions more rigid. Jimerson returned to Birmingham, downcast.

Two days following his departure, the Talladega Circuit Court enjoined and restrained him from "engaging in, sponsoring or encouraging unlawful street parades, unlawful demonstrations, unlawful boycotts, unlawful trespass, and unlawful picketing . . . and from conspiring to engage in [any of these activities] . . . and from doing any acts designed to consummate conspiracies to engage in said unlawful acts of parading, demonstrating, boycotting, trespassing and picketing, within the City of Talladega, Talladega County and the State of Alabama."

The injunction came as a shock. If Jimerson's attempts to mediate the Talladega dispute were sufficient to cause him to be enjoined, then he could not carry out his work on behalf of the council elsewhere in the state. He hadn't "conspired" with anyone about anything in Talladega. And, if attempting to make peace could be made synonymous with "engaging in, sponsoring or encouraging unlawful activities," then the young minister stood in jeopardy of going to jail merely for carrying out his daily duties as director of the council. Any communication or contact with Negro leaders involved in racial disputes could result in the accusation that Jimerson had assisted or conspired with the "agitators."

I discussed this aspect of the case with the circuit judge who had issued the injunction, Judge William C. Sullivan. He agreed that the scope of the order was limited to Talladega County alone and that Jimerson would not be held in contempt for any activities outside the county. But the problem remained that if Jimerson's activities could be interpreted as enjoinable in one Alabama county, he would be subject to the same action anywhere he traveled.

Could the peacemaker be enjoined in his work? As it applied to Jimerson the injunction seemed to me to be a broad-gauge effort to shoot down anything that moved in the underbrush of racial discord. Along with others, Jimerson was named as co-conspirator with the president, the faculty and the entire student body of Talladega College. He had neither met nor known, at the time his trial began, nor even at its end, most of the persons with whom he had allegedly conspired to foment racial strife in Talladega County. My own investigation of the case convinced me that, regardless of any constitutional question concerning the student's right to demonstrate, in Jimerson's case he had in fact spent his time with the Negro demonstration leaders *trying to persuade them to stop demonstrating.* I learned that his advice was not only disregarded but in some cases resented. He was, after all, "an outsider."

Here then was the classic case of the man-in-the-middle, fair game for both sides. But the Negro side merely ignored Norman Jimerson. The white side regarded him as an apostate to the Caucasian faith and dealt with him as societies have dealt with apostates. He was cast out, to be shunned at best, pilloried at worst. Once again my enthusiasm for fighting what I knew to be the good fight was chilled by a realization of what happened to those who dared swim against the current of conformity. The age-old fear of ostracism, of being not merely an outsider, but an *outcast* from your own community, has killed more free spirits than fear of physical harm. The idea that I might be physically endangered by the nature of my cases had frightened but never impressed me up to this point. After all that was a risk that had to be accepted. After a while, telephone threats and scrawled notes swearing violent retribution, if not discounted, can at least be taken in daily stride. But the social isolation being suffered by Norman Jimerson was something else again. I had always been gregarious, priding myself on knowing more Birmingham people on first-name terms than any six lawyers my age knew in aggregate. Controversial, true—but still a man blessed with many friends. I even took some pride in believing that my friendship with large numbers of people, big and small, gave me a kind of social credit-in-the-bank that permitted me to take on controversial matters. But I knew that this credit might run low or in fact might be overdrawn someday. And when matters reached that point, what would my reaction be if my church or some organization asked me to leave in order "to avoid embarrassment and trouble," as Norman Jimerson had so often been told?

I had already experienced a degree of isolation during political campaigns. But that was politics, and in a political campaign the roles of prophet and pariah are often interchangeable on sudden notice. These just weren't my years for public politicking, I had concluded. But if this experience had in truth been a harbinger of a wider ostracism to come . . .

In Norman Jimerson I saw a human being, a good but a

misunderstood human being, lose his social moorings. He was not merely cut adrift from the white society of the community, but neither did he have any place in the Negro society for whose cause he had sacrificed himself. The Negro involved in the racial struggles of the Deep South stands with his community. But the white Southerner who champions the Negro cause may be an outsider both to his own and to the Negro community.

Norman Jimerson and others charged with conspiracy in organizing street demonstrations in Talladega, Alabama, went on trial October 8, 1962. After two weeks of testimony, the case against Jimerson was dismissed by the State of Alabama. Evidence introduced during the trial was wholly insufficient to support the charge that the peacemaker had in fact been engaged in any activity other than trying to make peace.

As I walked out of the Talladega courthouse, several local whites were congregated on the steps. "Look," said one. "There goes that nigger-lovin' son of a bitch from Birmingham."

This time I knew they weren't talking about one of my clients, but about me.

CHAPTER

XII

Welcome Home, Bob Zellner . . .

THE STUDENT NON-VIOLENT COORDINATING COMMITTEE
is the guerrilla arm of the Negro equal rights movement.
It recruits its membership from the ranks of the young, from
college students and recent graduates. Its goal is the organization of a militant Negro movement in the isolated rural towns
of the Deep South. Voter registration is the lever by which it
hopes to raise Mississippi Delta and Alabama Black Belt
Negroes to equal status.

My introduction to this organization came early in 1963
when I undertook the defense of John Robert Zellner, white,
twenty-three-year-old son of a Methodist minister. He was a
SNCC "field secretary," civil rights movement parlance for
"organizer." An Alabama native, he had graduated from
Huntingdon College, a Methodist-supported institution in
Montgomery. As a leader in the SNCC movement, Zellner
wore an arrest record as a badge of honor. He was known from

McComb, Mississippi, where he had been jailed for participation in demonstrations—to Albany, Georgia, where he had been a Freedom Rider—to Baton Rouge, Louisiana, where he had been indicted as an anarchist—to Talladega, Alabama, where he had been among those charged with conspiring to violate the local trespass laws.

On January 5, 1963, Zellner arrived in Montgomery just in time to be the first person arrested on orders of the Wallace administration. He had to work at the honor. He made it inside the Montgomery county jail a full six days before George C. Wallace took office as governor of Alabama.

George Wallace had looked forward all his life to the day when he would be inaugurated governor of Alabama. He came to the mansion by a long, arduous route. His youth had been shaped by poverty. The mortgage on his family's farm had been foreclosed in 1937, but five years later persistence and hard work earned him a law degree from the University of Alabama. A new lawyer, his first days following graduation found him driving a dump truck to make ends meet. Newly married, he, his wife Lurleen, and their first child rented and lived for a time in a converted chickenhouse. In 1943, serving in the Army Air Force, he was felled by spinal meningitis and hospitalized. But he saw action overseas and returned to Alabama to launch a career in politics.

In 1946 he was elected to the state House of Representatives from his home county of Barbour. He went to Montgomery and served as a legislative lieutenant for Jim Folsom, then in 1952 went back home and won election as circuit judge.

Wallace's journey through the thicket of state political

ideology and factionalism was every bit as tortuous. As a
Folsomite, he was considered a liberal, by some even a dangerous Populist radical. Attending the Democratic national convention as a delegate in 1948, he refused to join Alabama's
Dixiecrats in their walkout protesting the convention's civil
rights plank. But by 1953 the young man who by that time
prided himself on his sobriquet "The Little Judge" (in the
manner of his boyhood idol, Governor Bibb Graves of Barbour County, who had been called "The Little Colonel")
was issuing an injunction against the removal of segregation
signs on railroad terminals. He then traveled the route from
being Folsom campaign manager in the 1954 gubernatorial
race to becoming himself a hard-line segregationist candidate
in 1958; reversed field again in the run-off with Patterson to
become thought of by some as the "liberal" candidate fighting
the Klan; and swung back to outflank the field as a hard-liner
in 1962.

Wallace was by no means an early favorite to win in the '62
campaign. Some considered his political road at an end. He
was up against Big Jim, his former mentor, who took away
a large share of Wallace's courthouse crowd support. He was
also up against some major league competition in garnering
segregationist votes. Bull Connor, Albert Boutwell and Mac-
Donald Gallion owned strong records on the Issue. And there
was a new face, that of State Senator Ryan DeGraffenried of
Tuscaloosa, to compete with Wallace's image as a young man
with get-up-and-go. But Wallace was a scrambler, and having
come this far he was not to be denied on this last mile. Relentlessly he bore down on his segregationist theme, drowning out
the voices of his competitors in that area with his "stand-in-
the-door-and-go-to-jail" pledge. Relentlessly he bore down

on the bread-and-butter Populist issues of every Alabama campaign—the welfare programs, the pension promises, better roads, improved education, industrial progress. He earned at least a draw with Big Jim in projecting himself as the po' folks candidate.

In the primary, Wallace led the field with DeGraffenried running second. Folsom was now out of it, beaten by segregation and himself and, as with all men and causes, by time. The "clean, green breeze" of 1946 had now become the calm of 1962. Two young men were to fight it out for the governorship.

But it was really no fight at all. DeGraffenried had come from out of nowhere in state politics to a run-off position, but he was still relatively unknown compared to Wallace. Now Wallace, like Patterson four years before, had the primary lead and the Issue on his side. He ignored DeGraffenried—except to point out that Eastern newspapers had termed his opponent the "moderate" candidate of the city folks—and hammered away at his successful first primary theme. The Little Judge won overwhelmingly. The road had been long but George Wallace had reached the mansion. But for an ambitious young man there are no destinations—only vantage points.

Bob Zellner was arrested on the campus of his alma mater, Huntingdon College in Montgomery, and taken to the Montgomery county jail. Originally told by his arresting officers that he would be charged with "conspiracy against the State of Alabama," the Alabama-born SNCC organizer was held incommunicado and without a warrant being sworn out against him for several hours.

"Confidential information" had been circulating among the incoming governor's friends that Zellner had come to Montgomery to organize desegregation demonstrations coincident with the inauguration. Under interrogation Zellner refused to answer questions until he had an opportunity to talk with his lawyer, Montgomery attorney Clifford Durr.

Meanwhile two of outgoing Governor John Patterson's lieutenants met with him at the stately governor's mansion. There they told Patterson that Zellner had been arrested without a warrant. A state investigator had been asked to swear out a warrant, but Zellner apparently had violated none of Alabama's laws. Patterson, the former attorney general from Phenix City, clearly had no sympathy for an integrationist like Zellner. "But I grew up in a town where you always worried about somebody arresting you or your friends on trumped-up charges," he told the outgoing head of the highway patrol. John Patterson had seen men grow gray fighting cases like this. "We'll have nothing to do with it," Patterson told his callers. "Let them swear out their own warrants."

Since no other charges had been filed against him, Zellner was taken to the city jail, where a warrant for his arrest was sworn out by a Montgomery policeman. The charge? Vagrancy.

The following morning he was brought before the city recorder, where he heard evidence presented regarding his alleged plans to disrupt the Wallace inaugural. At the conclusion of the testimony, Zellner's sentencing was delayed one day. He was taken back to jail.

Meanwhile, the young SNCC organizer's wallet had been picked up by authorities at the site of his arrest on the Huntingdon campus. The wallet contained eight dollars and a pawn ticket showing the purchase of a camera and lens from the City Pawn Shop. As matters developed, this would be the one-way ticket with which Montgomery police authorities would try to send Zellner to the penitentiary.

The owner of the pawn shop, reading in the next morning's *Advertiser* of Zellner's arrest, contacted police to find out whether they had recovered his camera and lens. He was worried because he had taken Zellner's personal check for $85 in payment for the camera. The police reported that Zellner did not have the camera and lens at the time of his arrest. The Atlanta bank on which the prisoner had drawn his check was contacted, and officials there said that, according to their records, Zellner's bank balance was not sufficient to cover the check. Now a second warrant was issued, this time on a charge of acquiring property under false pretense, a felony. Possible sentence: ten years.

Wallace's inauguration took place January 14—without incident, as it were. Bob Zellner was brought before the Montgomery recorders' court again four days later, January 23. At this hearing Maury Smith, a deputy circuit solicitor, called to the witness stand, said that he had offered Zellner a settlement of his vagrancy case:

Q. (Mr. Durr): What recommendation did you say you would make to the Court? . . .
A. (Mr. Smith): My recollection is that if this boy . . . would leave Montgomery and cause us no trouble in regard to race matters, that we would recommend either to this Court or to the Judge presiding in the Circuit Court that he be given a $100 fine and a 30 day suspended sentence in the vagrancy case, and if that were agreeable we would ask the court to nolle pros. . . .

But Zellner had refused the compromise offer.

"Mr. Durr replied that having consulted with his client, that he was not in a position to accept that recommendation," Smith told the court. Zellner simply insisted he had not come to Montgomery to organize any demonstrations—at least, not this trip—and he would not agree to a settlement based on a warrant for "vagrancy" rising out of that accusation.

The court bound Zellner over to await action of the grand jury on the false pretense charge. On February 15, he was indicted. On the day before, St. Valentine's Day, vagrancy charges against him had been dropped, the prosecutor declaring that the city could "not sustain and support the charge of vagrancy against this defendant." But now Zellner was in serious legal trouble, faced with a felony charge in a hostile community. It was the worst kind of hostile community—a home town (of his college days) turned against him and everything he stood for. As events stood, it would have been more practical for him to have accepted the deputy solicitor's offer, back when it had been made; but it seems that no man —not even an unrooted, free spirit like Bob Zellner—can take lightly being told to stay out of his own home town. Now this natural instinct might mean long-term imprisonment.

Zellner's attorney, Clifford Durr, telephoned me to ask if I would undertake his client's defense in court. I had met Durr at a state Bar meeting but did not know him well. He was a close friend of Zellner and, although he had felt at ease defending Bob in the vagrancy case, the felony charge was a gamble for high stakes. Aside from his personal friendship—and the emotional strain involved in the defense of a friend—this could prove to be a taxing case physically. Durr wanted a younger man to serve on the firing line.

I had been following the case with interest, but the prospect of involvement in still another civil rights case had little appeal at this time. I had spent much of the previous year in controversy—too much, in fact, for the good of my law practice. I was very much aware that I needed a period of months to mend my fences with my regular clients.

Nevertheless, I soon found myself traveling down the new Birmingham-Montgomery highway to the capital, cursing both myself and Zellner. Zellner was a man in trouble—as much if not more trouble than any of my previous civil rights case defendants. A lawyer, no more than a doctor or a priest, can select the day of service, its place or the patient or parishioner.

Zellner was arraigned on February 19, 1963. Against the advice of Montgomery lawyers I raised the issue of systematic exclusion of Negroes from the grand jury venire. How well I knew their objections. A motion attacking the racial make-up of a county's juries may bring forth the ill will of the judge and other court officials. More importantly one of the jurors eventually selected to hear the case might bear the motion in mind with prejudice to the defendant. I sometimes caught myself worrying over these problems. But they often seemed more the creatures of rationalization than valid arguments. Whether hesitant over the motion or not I knew that Zellner had little, if any, good will left to be lost in Montgomery. And if the jury question was not raised now it would be lost forever. Bob would not be able to have a conviction reversed on appeal if his lawyer did not raise the proper questions at the proper time. My motion posed the question of whether a white defendant can properly question the exclusion of Negroes from the jury system. But my white client was a white *integrationist,* and my contention was that Negroes, if a part of the community of justice, might be expected to look upon his case with less antipathy than an all-white jury. Moreover, a flaw in the system is a flaw in the system, and if a jury is improperly constituted because it excludes Negroes in cases involving a Negro defendant, it is improperly constituted for a white defendant as well.

Not entirely unexpectedly, my motion was denied and the trial judge set the case for the following Wednesday, February 27.

The trial opened with Montgomery's modern, new courtroom crowded with the venire of prospective jurors. Four members were Negroes. Now an ironic incident occurred, one which temporarily baffled my client. The solicitor's office, with its challenges, eliminated three of the Negroes from participation on the trial jury. One lone Negro remained, yet the prosecution did not challenge him.

I turned to Zellner. "Do you know him?" I asked.

Zellner shook his head. "No, I don't," he replied. "Why?"

I had a single challenge left. After a moment's hesitation, I eliminated the lone Negro. Zellner looked at me as if I had just uttered the Klan cry. "Why?" he asked. "Why did you strike him from the list?"

"Because the state didn't," I told him. If the prosecution was willing to leave him on the jury, I was not. Later I explained to my client that simply because a Negro has a right to be a juror it does not follow that every Negro will make a favorable juror. I did not want the opportunity to prove my point.

The prosecution proceeded. There were few real facts in dispute. Zellner had purchased the camera and lens for $85, paying for it with the check drawn on the Atlanta bank. A photostat of his bank statement indicated that on the day he wrote the check his bank balance was deficient. But on the day following $200 had been deposited in the account. A telegram from the Atlanta bank to Montgomery police, stating that Zellner's check would have been honored if presented for payment, was introduced into evidence. The pawn shop operator had called the police about his camera and lens even before trying to negotiate the check. In fact, he had never made a complaint nor had he sworn out a warrant. All he wanted was either the check or the camera and lens—both of which were now exhibits in evidence.

Nearing the conclusion of our defendant's case, I was troubled about whether to put Zellner on the stand. This question can be crucial, but it is not always easy to answer. He had been involved in trouble and litigation throughout the South, and putting him on the stand would open the door to questions—and answers—that might inflame the jury. True, he would testify that he thought funds had been deposited to his account prior to writing his check—but by whom? By his employer, James Forman, SNCC leader. To white jurymen in Montgomery, Alabama, the idea of a white man working for a Negro might seem worse even than the procurement of property by fraud. I made my decision: the defense rested. Zellner did not take the stand.

The prosecution summed up its case in a dispassionate review of its evidence. I argued that there was no intent to defraud anyone. "How many hundreds and thousands of housewives on Thursday have bought groceries, knowing the paycheck was coming in on Friday?" I asked. Concluding, I attacked directly the real source of Zellner's difficulties. Yes, he was an integrationist, but "when the day comes in this state that a man who disagrees can be charged and convicted of a crime, we will all be in trouble."

The jury was charged by the judge and retired to consider its verdict. When the members reported back that they could not reach a decision at the end of the day, the court was adjourned until next morning and the long overnight wait began.

A lawyer's conclusions about the collective mind of a jury-with-case depend on much the same evidence as a medieval sorcerer's predictions of things to come: a witness looked this way and a juror wrinkled his brow; another witness had a raspy voice and a juror winced; this one looked me straight in the eye when I gave my concluding argument; that one glanced at the defendant.

What goes into a verdict? The prides, passions and prejudices of each of the twelve jurors, including their first or last impression of the defendant—not to mention his lawyer—and in a case like Zellner's, their individual reaction to community attitudes. In a case with racial overtones small things can become vital. Where do Negro spectators sit and how many are in the courtroom? Does the defendant speak, or nod, to any of them? How many white friends does he have in the courtroom, and what about his family? How is he dressed? And what about the lawyer? During the Zellner case one close friend of mine, a local attorney who earned his livelihood before Montgomery juries, bet another that he damned well would shake hands with me in the courtroom, in full view of the jury. But he lost his own bet—perhaps to win a case some other time. Only one Montgomery lawyer even spoke to me in front of that jury.

But there are lucky little occurrences, too. The newspapers can prejudice a community attitude against a defendant at times, but on the following morning when I read the Montgomery *Advertiser* at breakfast in the hotel, my spirits were buoyed by a single panel cartoon on the comic pages: a worried man at his desk at home was being shouted at by his wife; "Oh sure, it's *my* fault we're overdrawn! Has it occurred to you that maybe *you* underdeposited?"

The jury continued its deliberations throughout the morning. Then, in early afternoon, the panel returned to the courtroom to announce its inability to agree on any verdict. The judge ordered a mistrial; Bob Zellner was free. An all-white jury in Montgomery, Alabama, had disagreed and by that disagreement had granted him his liberty. The State of Alabama was to dismiss the felony charge and the only badge of honor Bob Zellner would carry away to commemorate his visit to his home town was a $25 fine for trespassing—on the campus of his alma mater, Huntingdon College.

Some weeks later I read in the Birmingham *News*, sandwiched in among news stories concerning George Wallace's activities in the state capital, a report that John Robert Zellner had been arrested in racial demonstrations in distant Danville, Virginia.

With the Bob Zellners of the world, going to jail doesn't matter much—what seems to matter is why you go there.

XIII

The Other Schoolhouse Door

I shall ask the Legislature to give me the right to assign pupils to schools which are threatened with integration. And when the court order comes, I am going to place myself, your governor, in the position so that the federal court order must be directed against your governor. I shall refuse to abide by any such illegal federal court order even to the point of standing in the schoolhouse door, if necessary. If they do not back down, the spectacle of a federal government treating the governor of a sovereign state like a common criminal by jailing him will in itself wake the American people up to the fact that the ultimate purpose of this bunch of political hypocrites is really to destroy every state capitol, every county courthouse and every city hall in America.

> —GEORGE C. WALLACE, Campaign Kick-off Rally, Montgomery, Alabama, March 10, 1962

This represents a new challenge for me. It's up to me to make good on it, and not necessarily for the sake of my race but for the sake of myself. This situation speaks very well for the City of Huntsville, the State of Alabama and the country as a whole. We realize there are many problems, but we believe we can work them out.

> —DAVE M. McGLATHERY, on the occasion of his registration at the University of Alabama Extension Center in Huntsville, Alabama, June 13, 1963

IN HIS OPENING CAMPAIGN SPEECH, George Wallace had promised he would go to jail before the federal government desegregated any school in Alabama while he was governor. In his inaugural speech he pledged "segregation today, tomorrow, forever." Both promises were to go unremembered on the bright, clear day in June, 1963, when The Little Judge traveled to the campus at Tuscaloosa to meet and back down before federal authority. He did not go to jail, and in this political instance "forever" meant three months.

Wallace had promised during his campaign that in his confrontation with the "Feds" Washington would likely back down "because the people of this country will not stand for the jailing of the highest official within a state." But Washington did not back down; the end result sought by the "Feds," the matriculation of Negro students at the University of Alabama, did come to pass. And it happened with never a pause in Wallace's shadow-boxing show of defiance—not from a federal penitentiary, as advertised, but from state capitols, county courthouses, city halls, university halls—anywhere an audience would gather to hear him relate his saga of the schoolhouse door.

But there was another schoolhouse door that June, a second University of Alabama entranceway where a Negro, Dave M. McGlathery, registered as a student without the fanfare or temporary delay of gubernatorial intervention. Along with James Hood and Vivian Malone, who had waited in a car out of camera range in Tuscaloosa, McGlathery, in upstate

Huntsville, was among the first members of his race to become a university student. Nearly a decade after my call to Autherine Lucy to tell her I hoped to help prepare the students at the university, I helped prepare the legal way for another Negro to do what she had attempted in vain.

My contact with Dave McGlathery began on a spring day in March, 1963, two months after Wallace had taken office. I had been asked to drive to Huntsville to meet two men who wanted to attend the University of Alabama as postgraduate students in advanced technology. Both were employees of the United States in missile research at Huntsville. They needed courses offered at the University Extension Center in order to perform their duties better and compete with fellow workers who possessed more academic training.

Our first meeting took place at the Huntsville residence of a Negro dentist, John Cashin, Jr. Dr. Cashin and his wife were leaders in the Negro community, and for an observer traveling from Birmingham to another city in Alabama the couple and their way of life were more than startling. The Cashin home was one street away from other homes—all equally new, modern and expensive—but owned by white families. In the Cashin side yard rested a cabin cruiser for jaunts on the nearby Tennessee River. The driveway held two automobiles—one a Rolls-Royce. Inside the home itself, I met several Negro and white couples—and was later to hear the Cashin children invited to a birthday party by a pert little white six-year-old. And conversation revealed that Dr. Cashin's dental practice included many white patients. Amazed, if not dumbfounded, I concluded that the geographical distance between Birmingham and Huntsville is ninety miles, but the actual distance could only be measured by the light years in which the nearby space center dealt.

Huntsville had been an old Southern town, like Mobile. The coming of the space age, and the U.S. government's development of Redstone Arsenal and the National Aeronautic and Space Administration Center had vigorously transformed the community, bringing in new people and a new way of life. Huntsville throbbed with the challenge not of the next day or even the next year, but the next decade.

I sat in the Cashins' comfortable living room and listened to McGlathery and Marvin P. Carroll as they told the stories of their attempts to enroll in the university.

Dave McGlathery was twenty-six, married, with no children. A native of Huntsville, he had graduated magna cum laude from the city's Alabama A. & M. College, a state-supported Negro institution. After graduation from college in 1961, McGlathery served in the data-processing section of the Transit Navigational Satellite System at the Naval Weapons Laboratory at Dahlgren, Virginia. He was now employed in the research projects division at the N.A.S.A.'s Marshall Flight Center in Huntsville as an applied mathematician in the field of space radiation shielding.

Carroll, married and the father of three, was a 1958 graduate of Howard University in Washington, D.C. He was employed in the electromagnetics laboratory of the U.S. Army Missile Command at Redstone Arsenal in Huntsville. He had been the first Negro selected by the Allis-Chalmers Manufacturing Company for its graduate training program in Milwaukee.

Both men told me that their reasons for wanting to attend

the University of Alabama were professional rather than ideological or political. There was nowhere else in the area to go for the courses they needed to advance them in their chosen fields. They did not want a spectacle, nor did they want out-of-state or civil rights groups to become involved in their admission. All they wanted was to enroll and go to classes—and they thought that a white lawyer, a University of Alabama graduate, and someone who knew the state and its officials could accomplish their end. They wanted me to guide them through the intricacies of their enrollment—and to do this without fanfare and, if at all possible, without a lawsuit.

To my knowledge, no white lawyer in the South had successfully brought suit to integrate a public school or state university. The professional challenge was great, greater than I had ever before attempted. There were, however, consequences to be considered. Involvement this time, I knew, would bring me to the brink of final cleavage with my home community. At any time, the representation of McGlathery and Carroll as clients for the purpose of enrolling them at the university would have been dangerous for a Birmingham lawyer. But, considering the community explosion which began shortly after I met the two, the assignment might now prove to be professional and social suicide.

The Birmingham *Post-Herald,* more than one year too late as usual, had joined the more progressive *News* and many of the city's business leaders in total disenchantment with the Birmingham City Commission. But there was only one way for them to oust Bull Connor and company from City Hall. Their terms did not expire until 1965. Hence, the city's form of government had to be changed. Several members of the YMBC were enamored of any opportunity to change the city's government.

Their chance came as an outgrowth of the reapportionment suit. The ten new house seats the Birmingham area gained by court order were to be filled in the November general election. A Democratic primary to select nominees was held in August. At each of the primary election polling places the voters were asked to sign petitions calling for a change in the form of government. Seventy-five hundred signatures were needed to insure a referendum on the matter. Most of Birmingham's wise heads had shaken "no" when the project was undertaken. It was impossible, they said, to obtain 7,500 signatures. But on election night when the signers were counted more than 11,000 names were on the dotted line. The November referendum was another battle over the "Southern way of life" but the proponents of change won.

What the Negroes came to call the Year of Birmingham had been triggered shortly after the election in early April, 1963, of Albert Boutwell as mayor under the new council form of government. Boutwell had defeated Police Commissioner Bull Connor in that bitter run-off of the campaign in which Tom King had lost his second bid for the mayoralty. The defeat of Connor, first in the referendum to change the form of city government, then in the mayor's race, was being talked up as the beginning of a new era in Birmingham community affairs. Now Connor was out—or was he? He refused to move from his office, and the new mayor and city council went to court, seeking an order to oust him. While the suit pended, Birmingham had two city governments, and soon had, as the local joke would run, "a King [Martin Luther], two Mayors and a parade every day."

Within days after Boutwell's victory, Negro leaders—including Dr. Martin Luther King—began a sit-in assault on the city's segregation laws. Bull, still wielding the community's police powers, ordered arrests and no retreat. Tensions slowly built, until with the arrest of King and local leader Fred Shuttlesworth, the doors of the Sixteenth Street Baptist Church opened and thousands of Negroes went out to take their protest into the streets. Nothing like it had ever been seen before—in Birmingham, in the South or in the country.

The next weeks were as frenetic as any in the history of any American community. Birmingham was a city deep in the shadow of a volcano, and the air was already dark with smoke and acid.

Now meetings between white and Negro leaders took place —interminable meetings, frustrating meetings, meetings filled with the misunderstandings and misconceptions growing out of the lost decades in which the city's interracial communications had been nonexistent. Community leaders came forward to ask the questions, hear the answers and discuss the problems which in past years they had shunted aside.

I participated in an early session. In a downtown church study a small group of whites including two business leaders met the Negro principals. The gathering was fruitless but written demands were presented to the white community. Later negotiations became formalized, each side having representatives charged with the duty of meeting, talking and reporting the results of conferences to their groups. From

[153]

time to time I was asked to advise some of the white negotia-
tors.

After agreeing to the desegregation of fitting rooms, lunch
counters, rest rooms and drinking fountains in a few downtown department stores, the business community met. This
time the problem was how to announce the existence of the
covenant. Birmingham's business leaders had been almost
unanimously captured by the city's age-old problem—no one
desired to speak for the business community. Consequently,
the solution was simple—let the Negroes do it. But, after de-
faulting on this responsibility, they wanted the statement
read by Dr. King to be properly worded. The agreement was
in writing but they worried over how it would sound when
announced. I drafted a statement. It began: "At last, the city
of Birmingham has reached an accord with its conscience. . . ."

One white business leader stated for the press that an agreement had been reached. He then left the city for the weekend
after being besieged with calls and threats. During the following week community curiosity about who was really involved
in the agreements with Negroes became so aroused that the
business leaders were forced to emerge from traditional roles
of anonymity. Their names were printed in the *News* and
Post-Herald for all of Birmingham to read. Even though their
names were revealed I thought that an "accord with conscience" would be very difficult for a city whose leadership
passionately did not want to lead.

Meetings and negotiations had proved fruitless until two
things occurred. Burke Marshall, head of the Civil Rights
Division of the Department of Justice, arrived in Birmingham. Rarely did he inject himself into the settlement of the
community's problem. But he was there and the presence of

the United States coupled with his quiet skill helped bring forth Birmingham's abstainers, its business community. And, secondly, the demonstrations were erupting with a new intensity. Adults were massed in the streets and children were leaving the classrooms and packing the jails. Chaos was loose in Birmingham. The time was short now—the volcano erupted for the city in the spring of 1963. Bull was beaten, but if Birmingham was to have a new era it seemed that it would have to be built on the smoldering ashes of the old.

Only by a chance of history did the climactic events in Birmingham coincide with George Wallace's accession to power. It was a crisis of the city's own making, and one which had been long years in the building. But the crisis of the University of Alabama was the child of a Wallace campaign pledge. Wallace the candidate's pledge to maintain segregation or go to jail was illusory, but now Wallace the governor would be forced to reconcile the reality of power with the illusion of the campaign.

In the meantime, I had agreed to advise and assist McGlathery and Carroll in their efforts to become students at the Huntsville University Center. At first, I would not commit myself to filing suit in court if that became necessary, though later I did so. The two men had not known each other until a few weeks before my meeting with them, but I discovered that their stories of frustrated efforts to enroll as students were closely parallel.

With the approval of their superiors at the space center, the two men had separately filed applications for admission to the graduate school. What followed was a war of time and nerves, a battle of paper. After delays, McGlathery was re-

jected for reasons technically growing out of a misunderstand-
ing regarding the taking of a multiple-choice test; and Carroll
was turned down because a transcript from Morehouse College, which he attended prior to Howard, had arrived at the
university too late for the processing of his application. Actually, McGlathery had twice applied for entrance, but had
himself withdrawn an original application to be admitted at
the winter session. With the Oxford, Mississippi, incident in
mind and a desire to enter the school peacefully he acceded
to requests to postpone his time of admission.

Despite Wallace's pledge, several factors were working in
favor of the two men's admission to the university. Their
academic credentials and projected courses of study could
not be challenged as easily as those in past Negro admission
cases. Moreover, although university authorities were under
the pressure of conflicting forces, the violence that had occurred at Oxford, Mississippi, the previous autumn had led
to a rethinking of the university integration problem on the
part of influential alumni and members of the board of
trustees. The University of Alabama, under the leadership of
President Frank Rose, had worked hard to repair its reputation damaged by the Lucy riots. Academic strides were being
taken—and the Research Institute at Huntsville was a key
element in the university's quest for national recognition.

Of the eighteen hundred students annually enrolled at
the university's Huntsville extension, five hundred—many
of them federal employees—took part in the graduate instruc-
tion program. And most of the graduate courses were fur-
nished under contract with the United States government.
Government employees at the space center, if they obtained

the approval of their employers—and both of my clients had received such approval—were entitled to attend university courses without charge under a contract between the university and the Department of the Army. The United States paid administrative costs of those courses that it desired taught at the extension and paid the students' tuition and fees. In addition, the university and NASA also had contract arrangements for employees of the space center. Thus, apart from its responsibilities under other federal court orders, the university had entered into an agreement to provide McGlathery and Carroll educational courses—and that agreement did not, as it could not, mention anything about the race of students to be admitted.

Events finally seemed to make the filing of a lawsuit a necessity if my clients were to become university students. Previously, I had hesitated about agreeing to carry the cause beyond administrative and into court channels. My concern had been personal. My deep affection for the university came into play. Now, in view of the tragedy enveloping Birmingham and the racial ferment coming to the surface throughout the state, I was convinced that the best interests of the university lay in the admission of McGlathery and Carroll as students. And the ideal time for their entry was in June, not September. For it was common knowledge that by September the public schools were to be desegregated in one or more Alabama cities. If Wallace was to persist in his dedication to a school door stand it would be far better that it take place at the college level and at a session of school where the enrollment was low and consisted in large measure of graduate students.

On May 8, I filed suit in the U.S. District Court to have McGlathery and Carroll admitted to classes for the summer term, beginning in June. Attorneys for James Hood and Vivian Malone had accelerated the requested date of their admission. They filed their own suit for admission to the main campus at Tuscaloosa for the summer session. On May 21 we went to court. Lawyers crowded around the counsel table and I made last-minute preparations of my argument. But there was no need for argument. The university was prepared to admit Miss Malone, Mr. McGlathery and Mr. Hood, but sought more time. The District Court, after refusing the request for further delay filed by the university, ordered Miss Malone, Hood and McGlathery to be admitted as students. Carroll had decided not to proceed with his request for entry, reducing to three the number of Negroes who would crack the racial barriers at the 131-year-old University of Alabama.

June 10 was the target date for enrollment. Now George Wallace had two schoolhouse doors to block, separated by many miles. The campaign illusion had developed into a logistical as well as a political dilemma.

The nation prepared for the battle of the schoolhouse door in Tuscaloosa. Television crews, commentators, reporters and representatives of the federal government descended upon the town. Profiles of the prospective students appeared in the nation's press. The student body of the university signed pledges not to commit violence. Coca-Cola bottles— potential weapons—were removed from on-campus dispensing machines. Identification cards were issued to those entitled to enter the university grounds, which were encircled by hundreds of highway patrolmen. Microphones were installed in front of a door and in Washington the President prepared to federalize the Alabama National Guard. The two Negroes waited in an automobile, off camera. The stage was set.

On Tuesday, June 11, George C. Wallace, now governor, stood in the door at stage center. Nicholas deB. Katzenbach, Deputy Attorney General of the United States, entered the scene from the right. The two Negro students waited in a nearby automobile, on camera.

Governor Wallace read from the prepared script. Mr. Katzenbach listened and then asked him to step aside. Governor Wallace allowed that he was not ready to leave. Mr. Katzenbach turned and walked away, leaving the blocked door.

Act Two was played after an intermission of three hours. General Henry Graham of the Alabama National Guard approached the governor, who had returned to his post at the door. General Graham, who had been federalized along with the rest of the Guard, now said that Governor Wallace would have to leave the set. Governor Wallace issued a victory statement, accepted General Graham's salute and marched away.

The door, now unstood-in, was open for the admission of Vivian J. Malone and James Hood. The curtain fell.*

Two days later, in Huntsville—in accord with an agreement which alleviated George Wallace's logistical problem— my client, Dave M. McGlathery, left work and drove to the

* According to press reports Alabama's state-supported institutions of higher learning were actually desegregated at Alabama A. & M. College in Huntsville, an all-Negro institution since its founding in 1875. Robert Muckel, twenty-nine, white, from Utica, Nebraska, enrolled on the morning

University Center. He walked from his car into the school alone. Nearby, federal officials, including Mr. Katzenbach, waited to see that the registration went off smoothly. The governor, having been turned down in a late request that McGlathery come to Tuscaloosa two days before so that only one stand would be necessary, passed up the opportunity for an encore before a North Alabama audience.

Inside the building, a Negro maid greeted Dave in subdued tones. And two janitors stopped work to watch. But there was really nothing special to see. Just another student registering at the University of Alabama.

---

of the governor's stand. The president of the college was quoted as saying: "We just assumed anyone coming to A. & M. would be a Negro. But we can't discriminate because of race or we would lose our grant funds."

"They've gone out of their way to make me feel at home," Mr. Muckel was quoted as saying. "I am not a martyr. I just came here to get an education."

A college administrator reportedly said: "All I can say is the same thing they said about James Meredith at Mississippi. Mr. Muckel is 'knowingly' our first white student, but we've had many students here over the years who you could not definitely say were white or Negro."

Muckel, according to reports, left his family behind in Nebraska because of "the housing problem." He "did not know it was this type of school when I accepted a grant here. When I found out I decided to come anyway." He was enrolled in the summer institute provided under a National Science Foundation grant and not as a regular summer session student; "so as far as we are concerned it might be said that there is no white student registered here" a college spokesman said.

XIV

The Bomb—and After

IT WAS THE CHILLY, OVERCAST MORNING of Sunday, September 15, 1963. People in the City of Churches had busily prepared themselves for Sunday school.

"You go on in, honey," Claude A. Wesley, the principal of a Negro school, told his fourteen-year-old daughter Cynthia as she stepped out of their black Mercury at the Sixteenth Street Baptist Church. "I'm going to get some gas and I'll be back in a minute."

There were four hundred people in church that morning. Twelve young girls crowded into the rest room downstairs near the auditorium. They were dressed as all little girls dress. Cynthia Wesley wore her white ruffled "Sunday best," with a red sweater draped over her shoulders.

Her father was standing at the service station two blocks

away. At 9:22 A.M. the bomb exploded. He heard the clatter of broken glass and brick, and the deep message of dynamite through the trees. He raced to the church.

People were pouring into the street, crying, screaming, frightened. Sarah Jean Collins, twelve, staggered from the hole in the building, her hands covering her blinded eyes and blood-streaked face.

A woman standing in glass in the street shrieked, "My God, you're not even safe in church."

Ambulances and a fire truck arrived. Some Negroes threw rocks at them. They searched through glass and rubble. They found copies of a kindergarten leaflet with the day's prayer: "Dear God, we are sorry for the times we were so unkind." They were splattered with blood. And there was a coloring book picture of a child, praying. The dress was crayoned red, the face black.

Claude Wesley searched for his Cynthia. They sent him to the hospital.

"They asked me if my daughter was wearing a ring," he said. "I said yes, she was, and they pulled her little hand out and the little ring was there."

Denise McNair's mother was in the church when the bomb went off. She searched for her daughter.

"Daddy, I can't find Denise," Mrs. McNair told her father, M. W. Pippin.

"She's dead, baby," he sobbed. "I've got one of her shoes in here. I'd like to blow the whole town up."

Four bodies were found: Cynthia's, Denise McNair's, and those of Carol Robertson, age fourteen, and Addie Mae Collins (Sara Jean's sister), fourteen.

One of the children had been decapitated, another had a hole in her head the size of a fist. The injured jammed emergency wards.

That's the way church was on Sixteenth Street in Birmingham, the City of Churches, on Sunday, September 15.

"Did you hear about the church?" someone said. "They killed four kids." The rush of words was like a physical assault. Children—in church. And there weren't any words; there was nothing to say. I just stared and felt the anger. There is a kind of anger that slowly wells up in a man. For years I had been living a part of this city, yet apart from it. And during those days and weeks and months of watching hatred build its empire there had been anger, the frustrating, quiet kind of anger.

In Mountain Brook we didn't hear the explosion. We had heard others, like the one at Bethel Baptist Church in December a year ago, when the children inside were rehearsing for their Christmas pageant.

At lunch, Mrs. Davis, who runs the delicatessen in our neighborhood, was on the verge of tears.

"What are we going to do? Little girls in a church . . ." Her voice trailed off.

A prominent businessman stopped at our table. "I'd kill him," he said. "If I knew who he was, I'd kill him." He left shaking his head.

But there were others talking that Sunday, and the events of the morning didn't seem to bother them.

Downtown Negroes and whites threw rocks at each other in the streets. An eagle scout on a motorbike shot and killed a Negro boy; a policeman killed another. A white man was struck with a brick and lay in the hospital seriously injured. An entire city stared down the barrel of violence. It had to be a nightmare. And this was my home.

Who Speaks for Birmingham? This was the title of a 1961 television documentary concerning the city's race problem. The title was inspired. No phrase or question could better sum up the city's history . . . or serve as its epitaph.

Who spoke for Birmingham? On the day of the church bombing, many voices spoke—but none to place the blame where it belonged: on a community heritage of racial intolerance and on all members of the community who, by sins of commission and omission, condoned that heritage.

The atrocity at the church had been presaged by months, years, decades of community complacency toward its central problem. The fuse had been prepared by community indifference to violence and threats of violence. The bombing had not been inevitable. It did not have to happen. As recently as six months before, in the storm of Negro protest that had burst forth from this same Sixteenth Street Baptist Church, we had been forewarned. We had been given time—and what had we done with it?

Even now, in the first hours of the city's shame, what were we doing? And in the weeks and months ahead, what were we to do? Was the killing of four children but one more incident in the city's violent history?

I recalled that the producers of the 1961 television documentary had had a difficult time locating spokesmen who would agree to go before the cameras. Few wanted to talk, and most of those who did spoke up only in praise of the community's history and "image." In truth, no one spoke for Birmingham—and no one could speak for a city in which everyone, individually and collectively, washed his hands of responsibility for what had happened, what was happening— and what would happen in the future.

No one could speak for Birmingham. But then, the city was not looking for a spokesman. It was looking for a scapegoat.

I could not speak for Birmingham—but I could speak to it. On the morning following the bombing I went to my office and began preparing my statement to be made before the Young Men's Business Club that noon. I wrote in anger and final intolerance for what I considered the community's blindness. The speech when delivered would be from the heart—I did not read it. But it was important that I organize my thoughts and set them to paper. Later, for publication, I would put them into final form. But now, with so much to say, punctuation seemed less important than the message itself. There was much to say. It was the message of one who loved his city, who had worked for his city, who had hoped for his city. But most important now was the need for someone to speak in protest not against the great wrong done by the bombers to the community "image," but against the great wrong we had all done to the victims and their families.

The telephone rang. I looked at the bedside clock. It was 5 A.M. of the morning after I spoke at the Young Men's Business Club.

"Is the mortician there yet?" asked a voice.

[165]

"I don't know any morticians," I answered.

"Well, you will," the voice said, "when the bodies are all over your front yard." The receiver clicked.

At 6 A.M. the telephone rang again. A different voice, but much the same message. And for the hours, days and weeks ahead it would ring again and again, at first threatening my life, later threatening my wife and child.

The word was out early that morning. I had stood up at the YMBC meeting and indicted our community.

Now, in the community's hour of crisis, it seemed I had been able to perform a service after all—by providing the scapegoat it needed to survive the weeks and months ahead. If the image had indeed been tarnished, the fault lay not with the community but with its critics. According to this logic, by speaking out I had done the community a wrong. This was the prevailing sentiment.

Why, they challenged, had I said, "Birmingham is dead?" The newspapers, in three-month editorial campaigns, reassured the community:

"Fly the Banners of Confidence," said the local press. Daily front-page declarations cited various community virtues including: "Birmingham is a religious city. Three out of every five families regularly attend church services . . ."; "Birmingham's Honeysuckle Hill is the finest section of Negro homes in the United States. . . ."

But for the failure to apprehend the bombers of a church and the killers of children within, or the bombers of homes— for these the Birmingham newspapers had no editorial banners.

But the newspaper's campaign found supporters: a local

business ran radio spot announcements declaring that Birmingham was not dead—his sales had been booming.

Why had I said, "Birmingham is guilty"?

The bombing of a church, the killing of innocent children can take place in any community, the newspapers assured their readers. But do atrocities take place in social vacuums? The ovens of Nazi Germany and the labor camps of Stalin's Russia could not have existed in the England or the America of the 1930's or 1940's or today. Nations and communities, by the standards of conduct they establish and which their citizens stand up and speak up to defend, create the social atmosphere which can breed atrocities—or respect for fellow man.

Birmingham was my home. Birmingham's people were my people. Years before, like other young men who loved their home cities, I had hoped for and committed my future to the building of a better community, for myself, for my neighbors, for our children; but all Americans are members of another community as well, and if I could not speak for or live with Birmingham I could perhaps speak for that larger community whose heritage is based on human dignity and human rights. This is the community toward which men and women throughout the world have turned in hope. Only by making the American hope a reality for all its citizens, white and Negro alike, can Birmingham realize its own.

If Birmingham and cities like it are to have hope, it must come from those members of the white community who are not afraid to succumb to conscience. There are too few of these people. There always are. But they are there. They go about their business until some circumstance or event, large or small, calls for commitment. For some this commitment may mean financial, social or political ruin. Some may escape the society's more stringent sanctions. Perhaps there will be no retribution. But, when he acts, the Southern white man can never be certain it will not mean his job, or community standing, or his physical safety.

Yet in Birmingham even today there is a plant manager who, while an assistant, shook hands with a Negro employee receiving his twenty-year service pin. He was admonished by his superior. But a short while later, when he became plant manager himself, he removed the factory's segregation signs from the drinking fountains and rest rooms. When protests were made and the signs surreptitiously raised again, he made an outspoken segregationist employee climb the ladder and remove them in full view of his co-workers. Three times someone wrote "Negro" above one of the fountains. Four times he had a crew paint over the word.

And there is a minister who, when wealthy and prominent members of his congregation demanded that his assistant be fired, told them that he, too, would resign; that his assistant must be allowed the right to speak out on any subject, including race. Both men stayed. And there is a state representative who stood young and alone in dissent and defeat as his colleagues shouted more segregation bills through the legislature.

And there is a local news commentator who, despite possible reprisals, four days following the death of President Kennedy said: "Daily we hear protests that Birmingham is not a dead city. That it is a vibrant one, full of promise for the future . . . a city that one day will outlive its reputation for violence and bigotry . . . a city ready to move forward. Yet, when school children applaud the assassination of the man holding the highest office in the United States, and this goes unmarked by reprimand, then it is time for the pall-bearers to ready for their task. . . ."

There is the man who hired a Negro secretary in down-town Birmingham. "Fire her or move out" was the ulti-matum. He moved.

And a law firm which, when asked why it moved from one building to another, answered: "Our Negro clients got em-barrassed riding in your segregated elevators." The elevator signs came down.

And there was a landlord who came to me once and told me that my neighbors in the building had complained be-cause I had given my key to Negro clients and told them to use the only rest room on my floor. I asked him what he had replied. "I gave them keys to the rest room on another floor," he said. "They didn't like it, but that's too bad."

No one knows who will next be called to commit himself or in what way. It might be someone like the tall and lanky soldier in Jackson, Mississippi, the one with the long South-ern drawl who told a white man assaulting Negro Andrew J. Young: "Man, if you wanta fight, fight me! I'm your size and I'm white."

There are clergymen, doctors, lawyers, reporters, business-men and labor leaders who, when put to the test, will pro-duce in the South a new day for themselves, for the nation and the world. I have told some of their stories. Other stories will never be told.

Many of the voices of freedom in our land have sounded

from the South—from Jefferson to the McGills, the Ash-
mores, the Hartsfields—and the university presidents who
speak up for their precepts, and the judges who speak up for
our society's concept of justice, and the ministers who speak
up for the brotherhood of all God's children. They are
there, waiting.

When will the others speak?

Epilogue

AFTER THE SPEECH there came a rush of mail, constant telephone calls, most of them encouraging, and many conversations in my office. A clergyman called—he was not guilty, and he wanted me to know it. Young businessmen came by the office to complain that I was doing the city a disservice, that I should stand silent and speak no more, that I might be forgiven if I'd only keep my mouth shut.

These were the identified dissenters. But there were the other voices, anonymous, in a city where killers were free.

"Mr. Morgan, we're going to put a bomb in your office or automobile," said one. Another called to threaten my child.

A client drove sixty miles to urge me to leave the city. "They'll shoot you down like a dog," he said. "I've got a place in the country where you can go with Camille and Charles and stay for a few days until this thing blows over."

An old friend telephoned and invited us to visit with his family. He knew Birmingham; he had lived there for years.

Two weeks after the speech we left for a rest, and from 1,000 miles away we reflected on the years in Birmingham. I pondered the words of some of our silent friends. "You've destroyed your usefulness here" was the phrase. Perhaps they were right. But what usefulness was there to destroy when those who sat in silence and, as they would have put it, "worked behind the scenes," accomplished nothing?

For years I had spent countless hours with themes for the discouraged: "We all have a future here"; "Things will get better"; "We can work the problems out"; "The people are changing"; "The city will grow in new ways and we'll have new people here, new ideas and opportunity for all of us and our children." Although a Democrat I had lent encouragement to those who wanted a Republican party in our state in the hope that political diversity would both cleanse our party and allow our area to grow and prosper. I had labored in court, in politics, in community affairs. I had insisted to those who were disillusioned, "We must stay here; this is where the battle will be won or lost."

Looking back on those hours spent trying to convince others to stay I now realize that I was really trying to convince myself. With each bombing I usually went on a tirade of: "I'm leaving this city. It's no damned good. There's no future here for me. It'll never change." Then in a few days I would simmer down and the spark of hope would flicker. But on September 15 they snuffed out lives—and hope.

While I was away the city's leaders embarked upon a new campaign extolling Birmingham's virtues. And to those who are not deeply involved in the struggles of community conscience the city has many virtues. Although there is disenchantment in watching men and their cities ignore their faults and praise their virtues, there should also be understanding. For Birmingham's leaders in their programmed telling of the "good things" about their city are also involved in an age-old delusion. They are trying to convince not merely the world but also themselves.

We returned to Birmingham. I called in five lawyers and turned over to them my furniture, my law books and my practice. I closed the office down. Charles said good-bye to his friends and found a new home for his beagles. Camille locked our house and the FOR SALE sign went up. There was no way for us to remain in the city of which I had been a part yet from which I had grown apart.

In my travels about America since the day we left Birmingham I have talked and corresponded with the young and old, the liberals and conservatives of many places. I now know that which I had always sensed. Birmingham is really a microcosmic study of the nation, its people merely average if sometimes bewildered Americans. In Birmingham the destructive forces of humanity got loose. In most of the nation they have been contained. But the conversation of the concerned in the North, in the cool comfort of 4:30 P.M. cocktails, tells me how much easier it is for them to worry over Birmingham than over New York. And when they say, "Don't leave, stay there and fight," I am tempted to ask them, "With what— sticks and rocks?" "All the good people are leaving," says the Northerner—often himself an expatriate of the South—from the vantage point of years of absence. And although the best

[173]

response might be: "How does one stay with a wife and child in the midst of a battlefield, in a struggle to eat and live, with forums closed and threats to everything you love?" the more tempting reply is: "When are you going to make up your minds to end your appeasement of bigotry? When are the voices across the land of the free to be raised in defense of honor and dignity and freedom in your own home towns? And, with respect to the South, when are you going to refuse to tolerate leaders who allow a part of one nation indivisible to deprive a portion of its people of the rudimentary fairness guaranteed by the constitution? For how long are you and this nation going to tolerate the abuse of American institutions? And while you engage in the debate over what to do about Birmingham will you also worry over your own employees and co-workers, your schools and neighbors and that ghetto on the other side of town?"

Every story does not have a happy ending. Bob Hughes attended college in Boston for language training. As he was driving through New York before departure for Southern Rhodesia his automobile was rifled. The clothing he purchased for his stay of several years (the church clothing allowance had been $400) was stolen. The place—Harlem. And when Hughes arrived at his post he discovered that the schools were racially segregated. There was no school for whites. His wife taught their children at home. And the other day he wrote from Salisbury, Southern Rhodesia: "Rioting this week in the townships here—mass arrests, burnings, police dogs, tear gas. We're rapidly approaching the precipice."

Dave McGlathery did not return to college in the fall, but

Bob Zellner did. Other Negroes have entered the University, and Dave will always know that they are following in his steps on what was once a lonely walk to school. Bob Zellner is married now and enrolled at Brandeis University, where he is studying for his master's degree.

Tom Reeves went to Harvard Divinity School and graduated cum laude. Pursuing graduate study at American University, he intends to teach and write in the field of ethics and foreign affairs after he receives his doctorate.

Dr. Henry King Stanford left Birmingham for the University of Miami. He is its president now.

Norman Jimerson eventually returned to the Presbyterian Church which he first attended. But he wonders if it is not time to move on now, his usefulness at an end.

Of the five lawyers who originally filed the reapportionment suit, only two now live in Birmingham.

Lou Mitchell and Lee Graham, the curate and rector of our church, who did speak out, have gone their separate ways to Florida.

Some stories have no ending at all. Men merely do the best they can wherever they are. As with life itself, men move on to new places, new problems. But some do not. Medgar Evers was assassinated in Jackson, four little girls were killed in Birmingham, and John F. Kennedy was felled in Dallas, all in what the Negroes will come to call "the year of Birmingham." Some who struggle for the American dream die in the midst of battle. Others, like the young girls in church, are killed before they ever have the chance to be a part of life.

Birmingham, like the giant cast-iron statue of Vulcan overlooking it from atop Red Mountain, has not changed. Most of its people go about their daily lives in a normal manner. They enjoy their children, hope for a good life for them, and work in the civic drives and projects in which all Americans work. They join Rotary or the local Lions club; they give to charity and attend church on Sunday. Some bowl, others play golf. They root for the home team and watch television, read the papers and serve their state and nation in the armed forces. They, like most men in most times and places, wish to be left alone. They neither approve of violence nor actively participate in it. They are in every sense of the phrase, as it is commonly used, good citizens. Many of them disagree with the course of the nation and its government. They voice this disagreement as they have a right to do. Even this they do quietly and privately. But, though good, they are passive in the face of the enemies of society. As with most men in most times and places they are at home and comfortable. And, if asked, they would say, "Everything's been pretty quiet here lately."

The people about whom you have read are no different from the men and women of the average American city. But the Hugheses, the Zellners, the Jimersons, and the Reeveses dissent, and in their disagreement have listened to the drum beat of their consciences. In times of stress they merely did what they felt they were supposed to do; nothing more or less. Each of those who disagreed knew fear and heartbreak. But to some men being true to what they know is right is more important than the comfortable life. No matter where they are—or in what time—they are the men who weave the fabric of America—always near the "precipice."

Yet as time dims the echo of the late-night calls, the

thoughts of jails and days of trial and violence, most of them will remember the more pleasant things. Football on the weekends, the friends they made, the nice homes, springtime, and the happiness of their children when they were young in Birmingham.

I know I will.